Praise for
Chazown

"It is depressing to consider how many people will go to bed tonight never having thought of how God wanted them to spend the day. As Craig points out, this is a deadly cycle that quickly culminates in a wasted life. *Chazown* reminds us of the brilliance of our God who carefully created us and empowered us for a life of purpose. I pray it rescues many from an eternity of regret and leads them toward the satisfying and meaningful life God intended."

—FRANCIS CHAN, best-selling author of *Crazy Love*

"Craig Groeschel dreams God-sized dreams. But he's also one of the most down-to-earth people I know. You can't get close to him without getting a vision infection. And his church, Life Church, is like a church on steroids. Creativity oozes out of every pore, leaving a trail for churches to follow if they want to impact culture. If you need a dose of vision, pop the *Chazown* pill."

—MARK BATTERSON, lead pastor of National Community Church, Washington DC, and best-selling author of *In a Pit with a Lion on a Snowy Day, Wild Goose Chase,* and *Primal*

"Craig Groeschel is a leading voice among the new generation of communicators. He knows how to articulate people's deeply felt needs, and—even better—to help them identify and pursue their God-given dream with passion and purpose."

—JOHN MAXWELL, author, speaker, and founder of INJOY Stewardship Services and EQUIP

"Need help hitting the bull's-eye of life? A better life? A more meaningful and purposeful life? Help is here—in what you hold in your hands right now. Craig Groeschel is a master at opening up life and letting light in. So if you want a clearer, sharper sightline, *Chazown* is the book for you."

—ROBERT LEWIS, pastor-at-large of Fellowship Bible Church, Little Rock, Arkansas, and founder of Men's Fraternity

"Craig Groeschel epitomizes innovation. He has caught the wave of what it means to reach the world for Christ and is leading a charge to challenge the status quo of doing church. *Chazown* will put you in orbit. So climb in, buckle up, and take this journey of a lifetime."

— BISHOP EDDIE L. LONG, senior pastor of New Birth Missionary
Baptist Church, Lithonia, Georgia

"Craig Groeschel has been able to lead one of America's fastest growing churches while still having a life and a healthy, loving family. Now he lets us in on the secrets of his crystal clear vision and laserlike focus. It's not magic. It's not incredible giftedness. It's Chazown. Let Craig show you the way to discovering God's unique vision and calling for your life and the simple steps of alignment that make God's Chazown your reality."

— LARRY OSBORNE, pastor of North Coast Church, Vista, California

"To know Craig Groeschel is to be overwhelmed with God-sized vision. He's brilliant yet always a learner. Successful yet humble. Confident yet God-dependent. A leader committed to helping others fulfill their purpose on this planet. Craig does not *talk* vision; he embodies it."

— DR. SAMUEL R. CHAND, leadership consultant and president
emeritus of Beulah Heights University, Atlanta, Georgia

"Finding significance and meaning in our confused culture is like finding your way on a dark, foggy night. You need light and a seasoned guide to help you. Thankfully, your guide, Craig Groeschel, has provided the lamp in *Chazown*. And the result is a clear vision for life's journey."

— ROBERT V. CUPP, teaching pastor of Fellowship Bible Church,
Northwest Arkansas

"Craig Groeschel and Life Church are on the 'bleeding edge' of what the church may look like in the not-too-distant future. I love their vision, passion, creativity, and willingness to share what they are learning. Craig is the kind of leader who creates enthusiastic followers of Christ who believe that the only limits are those of vision."

—Greg Surratt, pastor of Seacoast Church, South Carolina

"One explanation for the recent failure of so many institutions in America is the failure of imagination. One of the reasons for the expansion of creative ministries at LifeChurch.tv is that Craig Groeschel's imagination raises the ceiling on what otherwise might have been simply one more new mission. If you want to learn from America's most creative pastor of the twenty-first century, listen to Craig Groeschel."

—Lyle E. Schaller, parish consultant

"Craig has a fresh catalytic vision of what the church could be…a grace place oozing with creativity, laughter, and innovation! I believe Craig is a leader for the next generation church."

—Dave Gibbons, social entrepreneur, World Vision board member, and lead pastor of NewSong Multisites in Bangkok, Los Angeles, Irvine, and North Orange County

———

"My Chazown is summed up in the words: living the reality of Christ. This one statement, though simple at first glance, has revolutionized my life. My personal values, giftings, and experiences have led me to a passion for leading people to live the reality of Christ in every area of their lives. The lights are on! I see God's purpose for my life and how every area of my life can help me reach it."

—Brandon, age 32

"This past year my wife and I realized that because of debt and poor financial decisions, we were unable to respond financially when God called us to give, be active in missions, or whatever He asked. God used the message of *Chazown* to light a fire in us to be debt free quickly. We have already paid off one credit card, and we're on track to have all of our debts—including our house—paid off in less than six years!"

—Derrick, age 29

"One thing that Craig's teaching on Chazown has helped me to realize is, God doesn't waste time. It is apparent to me now that God is using all of my life experiences—personal and professional, good and bad—to accomplish His vision for my life. It has given me greater appreciation for some of the life experiences that if left up to me, I would have chosen not to go through. Plus I have a better understanding of how I can leverage all that experience for good where God has me today."

—JERRY, age 42

"As I documented my core values, gifts, and experiences, I prayed that God would reveal exactly what that meant for me. He answered my prayer. I am here to make a difference in children's lives! My mission is to partner with parents in providing children with the skills, experiences, and resources that will enable them to become fully devoted followers of Christ. As I have continued to pursue God's calling in my ministry choices, He continues to equip me for bigger things. I feel so blessed to be able to bring glory and honor to God each day by fulfilling His calling on my life."

—DEIDRA, age 28

"When I was in the midst of a job transition with different opportunities before me, I went back to what God revealed to me in my Chazown. One of my core values is relationships and fostering relational community through service. I am gifted in shepherding and leading. And I had lots of experience in working with teams of volunteers. This knowledge allowed me to see clearly that God was calling me to work in a very 'hands-on' environment. After a year I cannot imagine doing anything other than what I have the privilege of doing now."

—GINA, age 33

"God has shown me that my Chazown is be close to Him and show Him to the world through music and word."

—BRIAN, age 30

"A year ago my husband and I were homeless and unemployed with two little kids. Now, we *both* have jobs and have a home of our own. God is showing me that my Chazown is to be involved in children's ministry somewhere, somehow. So I have been serving at our church's LifeKIDS ministries. My husband and I have been so *blessed*. God truly is good."

—MISTY, age 30

"After a lifelong struggle with my thought life, Craig taught on Chazown. God spoke to me and showed me that my Chazown is to live free and lead others to freedom. For over four years now, I have been free from pornography and a weak thought life. And my marriage is richer than I ever imagined it could be."

—CHRIS, age 34

"After reading *Chazown,* God gave me the vision to get in better shape physically. The first thing I did was park in the south parking lot and use the stairs to get into the office. Then I walked on my lunch hour and changed my eating to include mostly vegetables, meat, and fruit. When I still wasn't losing as much as I set in my goals, I joined a health club and began swimming laps. I now swim twenty to twenty-two laps four days a week and absolutely love it! But I would have missed out on this blessing if I hadn't pursued what God was showing me. With God's help I will lose all the weight I set in my goal. He is good!"

—JOANN, age 52

"My Chazown is to use my talents and abilities to inspire those around me so that they will seek out and find the love and grace of Jesus Christ. But when I first realized that, I was sitting at a computer in my office, which just happened to be an isolated room. And I am such a 'people person'! My work situation then almost seems funny to me now, but at the time my heart was sad. God clearly said, *With your life experiences and personality...I have clearly called you to more than this.* I followed His lead, and now I am leading others and building relationships with new people every day."

—TONI, age 36

"I had a vision to present a vehicle safety presentation to young drivers, but always found an excuse not to start it. When God showed me my Chazown, I realized that I must no longer delay, and I began to put my vision into action. It took me approximately two years to put a vehicle safety program together. But my presentation has won positive feedback."

—BARRY, age 41

"You always hear of these great stories of people getting debt free and how they have been set free from financial burden, but I wondered how it would ever be my story. More than one hundred thousand dollars in credit card debt, student loans, medical bills—you name it, we were under it. Then came *Chazown*! With the help of *Chazown* and three years of increasingly good decisions, we finally were able to celebrate becoming debt free this year!"

—DAVID, age 35

"The focus of my life was always job and performance, and the results were predictable—stress in my marriage, distance from my family, and burnout at my job. God showed me that my real Chazown is first of all my wife and family and then letting Him use my talents and abilities to be in mission. Today, my marriage couldn't be better, and my ministry is more meaningful and satisfying than it ever has been."

—DANNY, age 47

CHAZOWN

CRAIG GROESCHEL

CHAZOWN

**Define Your Vision, Pursue Your Passion,
Live Your Life on Purpose**

MULTNOMAH
BOOKS

CHAZOWN
PUBLISHED BY MULTNOMAH BOOKS
12265 Oracle Boulevard, Suite 200
Colorado Springs, Colorado 80921

All scripture quotations, unless otherwise indicated, are taken from the Holy Bible, New International Version®, NIV®. Copyright ©1973, 1978, 1984 by Biblica, Inc.™ Used by permission of Zondervan. All rights reserved worldwide. www.zondervan.com. Scripture quotations marked (KJV) are taken from the King James Version. Scripture quotations marked (NASB) are taken from the New American Standard Bible®. © Copyright The Lockman Foundation 1960, 1962, 1963, 1968, 1971, 1972, 1973, 1975, 1977, 1995. Used by permission. (www.Lockman.org). Scripture quotations marked (NLT) are taken from the Holy Bible, New Living Translation, copyright © 1996. Used by permission of Tyndale House Publishers Inc., Wheaton, Illinois 60189. All rights reserved.

Italics in Scripture quotations reflect the author's added emphasis.

Trade Paperback ISBN 978-1-60142-313-9
eBook ISBN 978-0-307-56278-4

Published in the United States by WaterBrook Multnomah, an imprint of the Crown Publishing Group, a division of Penguin Random House LLC, New York.

MULTNOMAH and its mountain colophon are registered trademarks of Penguin Random House LLC.

Library of Congress Cataloging-in-Publication Data
Groeschel, Craig.
    Chazown : define your vision, pursue your passion, live your life on purpose / Craig Groeschel.
— 1st ed.
       p. cm.
Includes bibliographical references (p.   ).
    ISBN 978-1-60142-313-9 — ISBN 978-0-307-56278-4 (electronic) 1. Christian life.
2. Decision making—Religious aspects—Christianity. 3. Dreams—Religious aspects—
Christianity. 4. Self-actualization (Psychology)—Religious aspects—Christianity. I. Title.
    BV4501.3.G75 2010
    248.4—dc22+
                                2010021432

Printed in the United States of America
2015

10 9 8 7

SPECIAL SALES
Most WaterBrook Multnomah books are available at special quantity discounts when purchased in bulk by corporations, organizations, and special-interest groups. Custom imprinting or excerpting can also be done to fit special needs. For information, please e-mail SpecialMarkets@WaterBrookMultnomah.com or call 1-800-603-7051.

CONTENTS

PART 1: SEEING CLEAR TO THE END
Why you need a new kind of vision

1   Your Final Chapter 3
2   Desperate for Vision 5
    You're the Author: Plan Your Epitaph

PART 2: CIRCLING THE TRUTH
Where to look for your own Chazown

3   Discovering Your Personal Vision 19
4   University of Chazown 21
5   Graduation Day 23

CIRCLE ONE: CORE VALUES 25
6   Hitting the Right Target 26
7   Spanning the Values Spectrum 29
8   Why Do They Do It? 31
9   The Anger-Bliss Factor 34
10 Unverified Values 36
11 Vacillating Values 38
    You're the Author: Your Core Values

CIRCLE TWO: SPIRITUAL GIFTS 41
12 Keira, Red with Pie 42
13 Doing Is Believing 45

14   Use It or Lose It 48
     You're the Author: Your Spiritual Gifts

CIRCLE THREE: PAST EXPERIENCES 52
15   It All Happened for a Reason 53
16   Mining Meaning from the Past 55
17   Eyes to See 57
     You're the Author: Your Past Experiences

PART 3: A DREAM IN DEED

How to name your Chazown and where to start

18   Three-Part Harmony 63
19   Perfect Fit: A Case Study 65
20   The Chazown Community 68

NAMING YOUR CHAZOWN 69
21   Closing In on Your Chazown 70
22   Impossible Mission *Possible!* 72
23   Of Course I Know Where I'm Going! 74
24   God Loves You (and Everyone Else Has a Wonderful Plan
     for Your Life) 76
     You're the Author: Your Purpose Statement

MOVING FROM VISION TO ACTION 80
25   Making It Up as I Go 81
26   Even God Thinks It's a Good Idea 83
27   How to Swallow a Moose 85
28   The Secret of Long-Distance Dreaming 86
29   Game-Winning Goals 88
     You're the Author: Your Short-Term Goals
30   The Very Next Step 91
     You're the Author: Your Very Next Step

PART 4: THE FIVE SPOKES OF CHAZOWN

Where you need to succeed "small" so you can succeed big

31 Picture This 97
32 Speaking of Spokes 99
33 Total Success 104
   You're the Author: Self-Inventory in the Five Fundamentals

FIRST SPOKE: RELATIONSHIP WITH GOD 109
34 Like Fish Need Water 110
35 The Accidental Disciple. 112
36 What's Your Temperature? 114
37 The Answer Is Already Yes. 116
38 You Can Get Closer to God. 117
   You're the Author: Your Relationship with God

SECOND SPOKE: RELATIONSHIPS WITH PEOPLE 123
39 Observations Along the Path 124
40 Viewing People with Purpose 126
41 Chazown and Good Company 128
42 As Good as It Gets? 130
43 Biblical Bridge Repair 133
44 Good Friend, Bad Friend. 135
45 Dropping Dead Weight. 137
46 The Journey Back 139
   You're the Author: Your Relationships with People

THIRD SPOKE: FINANCES. 143
47 Disaster Down Under 144
48 The Spiritual Side of Money 146
49 Chazown and Cash 148
50 You Can Turn Around. 150
51 Values, Vision, Victory. 152
52 Chazown with Legs 155

53 Getting to There from Here 157

54 It's Gotta Hurt 160

You're the Author: Your Finances

FOURTH SPOKE: HEALTH AND FITNESS 163

55 Fast Food for Thought 164

56 Staying Alive for God 166

57 Myopic Me-Management 168

58 Chazown in the Kitchen 170

59 Every Body Needs a Little Love 172

60 "Property of God" 175

You're the Author: Your Health and Fitness

FIFTH SPOKE: WORK 179

61 Getting to Why 180

62 Labor's Love Lost 182

63 The Ladder at the Top of Everest 185

64 Meaning in the Mundane 187

You're the Author: Your Work

PART 5: FROM HERE TO ETERNITY

Why you can't realize your Chazown alone

65 A New View of You 195

66 Hazards Ahead 197

67 We're All in School 198

68 Moved by Accountability 200

69 Different Kinds of Dropouts 202

70 Fork in the Road 204

71 Tell Me When I'm Wrong 206

72 Help Me When I'm Weak 207

73 Surprise Comeback 208

74   Living for the Second Embrace 210
     You're the Author: Your Accountability Plan

END MATTER
75   Already Living with Regrets? 215
76   My Part Is Finished—Yours Is Just Beginning 218
     You're the Author: My Chapter One

     Chazown Conversations 220
     Appendix A: Learning from Past Experiences 227
     Appendix B: Clarifying Your Core Values
        and Spiritual Gifts 232
     Notes 236
     Acknowledgments 237

PART 1

SEEING CLEAR TO THE END

Why you need a new kind of vision

YOUR FINAL CHAPTER

Most people take a long time to die.

(This is no way to start a book, you say.)

But think about it. There are those few who go suddenly. Accidents. Heart attacks. Gang shootings. A soapy slip off the edge of the tub. But for you, chances are that at the end of your life, you will die in bed. Waiting.

And while you wait, you will very likely have days, weeks, even years to think, to look back on your life.

Imagine yourself there, lying in bed and reflecting. Reading back through the chapters of your life story.

What did my life add up to?

Did I really matter?

What did I live for?

Who will remember me?

What will they say about me when I'm gone?

Why was it important that I existed?

So many questions. So much time. Will you lie there with no regrets? Some regrets? Nothing but regrets?

Imagine.

Or not. I mean, you'll probably have time to think about it when you get to that bed. So you could just wait. (Millions do.) See what comes. Wait until the final pages of your life story to see how it reads to you then.

> Imagine yourself there,
> lying in bed and reflecting.

But that's no way to end the story of your life.

Here's one more thing to think about: the decisions you are making today are actually making the bed you will lie in while you wait to die.

Which is why I wrote this book. To help you see your life differently, to see it the way your Creator saw it before you were born. And to live it with purpose and passion.

Starting now.

DESPERATE FOR VISION

I'm going to let you in on a secret. From this point on, to the end of the book, I'm winging it. That's right. I'm making it up as I go. I didn't have time to think through anything except the first few pages—thank you for reading this far—and the publishers needed the book right away.

But stay with me.

Keep reading.

If I accidentally say something good, you'll find it.

And now for another secret: What I just said? I was kidding.

That's no way to write a book.

But what if I had written this book without any forethought or preparation? If I did, you'd be kicking yourself for wasting your money and your valuable time. I wouldn't think of writing this or any other book without preparation, and neither would you.

But the greater and all-too-real tragedy is that so many in my generation are going through life without a vision, a big idea, a plan for their lives. I've found that if you ask people, "What is your vision for life?" you'll get answers like:

"I want to be rich."

"I want to be famous."

"I want to eat everything I want without getting fat!" (Someone actually told me that.)

But those aren't visions or big ideas for a life. They're substitutes for the real thing. They're glittery placeholders. They're excuses to allow us to continue to drift.

For the most part, people just stumble halfheartedly through life hoping tomorrow will be better than today. No plan. No dream. Mostly just existing.

Hoping for a break. They just keep turning the pages of their life story, one after the other, until they get to the final chapter.

And then…it's time for bed.

Death is a topic most people don't like to think about. As a pastor, I spend a lot of time helping people deal with it. Life-threatening illnesses. Sudden accidents. Funerals. Grieving families.

After a death, I always ask the family to tell me what was good in the life of the deceased. The answers are revealing.

Some families start talking and can't stop. They cry and laugh, relating story after story of a person who touched their lives, or gave their world meaning and hope. They celebrate a legacy. To them, the person now dead lives on as a shining light, an unforgettable example. A hero. A gift.

> So many in my generation are living without a vision, a big idea for their lives.

Other families fall into an awkward silence. They each seem to hold their breath. They stare at the floor. I know what they're doing—they're trying to come up with something honorable and good to say. They're glossing over pain, explaining away failures. Sometimes they start to speak, but…

I hate those silences.

Every life story, the good and the not-so-good, reinforces one central principle:

KEY THOUGHT
Everyone ends up somewhere. But few people end up somewhere on purpose.[1]

FEARFULLY AND WONDERFULLY MADE

The great news is that anyone can discover meaningful life direction. Everyone can end up somewhere on purpose. Not just the remarkably talented or fortunate. You. Me. Everyone.

The Bible makes it clear that we were designed from the start to live for a unique reason. For a dream. A big idea. A personal mission. That's because you and I are made in the image of a forward-looking, purposeful God. In Isaiah 46:10, He said, "I make known the end from the beginning, from ancient times, what is still to come. I say: My purpose will stand, and I will do all that I please."

In other words, before God starts something, He is certain of the outcome.

And God's map of history includes a unique plan for *your* life. In Psalm 139:13–16, David wrote:

> You created my inmost being;
>> you knit me together in my mother's womb.
> I praise you because I am fearfully and wonderfully made;
>> your works are wonderful,
>> I know that full well.
> My frame was not hidden from you
>> when I was made in the secret place.
>> When I was woven together in the depths of the earth,
> your eyes saw my unformed body.
>> All the days ordained for me
>> were written in your book
>> before one of them came to be.

Did you catch the amazing truth in those lines? God created you with a divine undertaking in mind. Before you were born, God knew you. And He knew what He wanted your life to be like.

That's why God calls us to live on purpose, keeping the end in view. And what's more, He invites us to seek Him in order to learn what His perfect plan is for our lives. Then, with that plan in mind, we can reach His and our greatest dreams. Anything less is a mistake, a lie, and a ripoff.

> God calls us to live on purpose, keeping the end in view.

Of course, living out your personal purpose, reaching for your God-given dream— that all sounds fine. But life happens. Bills pile up. Problems press in. We're blasted every day by a hundred media messages that tell us what we *really* need to do—the one thing that would change our lives—is buy a new truck. Or get to the mall. Or drink lite beer.

You talk about purpose…

If we're not careful, we can fall dreadfully behind, trying frantically to catch up, trying to accomplish…absolutely nothing.

But it doesn't have to be that way.

MADE FOR THIS

I'll bet your life is busy. Mine is too. For me, raising six children is challenging enough. Add to it the task of leading a large church with multiple campuses, and I often don't know if I'm coming or going.

My friends ask, "Craig, how do you do it all? Aren't you afraid you'll burn out?" What they really mean is, *Are you sure you're not heading for the psych ward?*

I can say with all honesty that my job and my family are never burdens. Sometimes I get tired. But I'm nowhere near burnout.

Why? Because this is what God created me to do. I have no doubt about it. I'm wired for this. This is the vision God put in me. And when God gives you His vision, He also gives you the ability to get it done. When you're living God's vision for your life, you spring out of bed with excitement. When someone asks if you like what you do, you shout "I love it!"?

But, Craig, you might ask, *will God give me a vision?*

Absolutely. I'm certain of it. In fact, the Bible tells us that vision is critical to our very survival:

> K EY THOUGHT
> "Where there is no vision, the people perish"
> (Proverbs 29:18, KJV).

This is the most important statement from Scripture that I will quote in this book. It's so important, in fact, that it is the source of the book's title.

WITHOUT CHAZOWN

The word *vision* comes from the Hebrew word *chazown* (pronounced khaw-ZONE). Not to be confused with *cassonas,* which is Spanish for underwear.

Chazown starts with a letter that doesn't exist in English. It's not the *ch* sound in *cheesecake*. You pronounce it by making a hacking sound at the back of your throat, like you're hawking and getting ready to spit.

Try it. Say *khaw-ZONE.*

And again. *Cha-ZOWN.*

Well, you'll get better with practice. (Incidentally, you may need to wipe off the page before you go on.) But more important than the pronunciation is the word's meaning. It means "dream" or "revelation" or "vision."

You'll notice that Chazown is frequently represented in this book by a spiral, or swirl. It stands for the energy, focus, and creativity that are released when you pursue your personal vision.

Chazown

Cha-ZOWN.

Where there is no Chazown—no dream, no revelation, no vision, no sense of our created purpose—we perish.

Where there is no vision that you were created to have a growing, life-long, and personal relationship with your Creator, your inner being withers and dies.

Where there is no vision that you have been placed on earth to matter deeply to other people, and reveal God's love and power to them, you live in loneliness and your relationships perish.

Where there is no vision for a godly family, you have a 50 percent chance of ending up divorced.

Where there is no vision that your body is the temple of God's Spirit—property on loan from Him—your physical health slips away. Your exuberance fades.

Where there is no vision for a financially wise lifestyle, you can live in the richest country on earth and still be drowning in debt.

Where there is no vision for meaningful work, people live for five o'clock. They really just exist. Their goal is to survive—to pay bills, stay married, keep the kids out of jail...

But you and I were made for so much more.

ONE LONE CHAZOWN

Imagine one man with one dream.

> I have a dream that one day this nation will rise up and live out the true meaning of its creed: "We hold these truths to be self-evident; that all men are created equal."
>
> I have a dream that one day on the red hills of Georgia, the sons of former slaves and the sons of former slave owners will be able to sit down together at the table of brotherhood....
>
> I have a dream that my four little children will one day live in a nation where they will not be judged by the color of their skin but by the content of their character.
>
> I have a dream today....
>
> I have a dream that one day every valley shall be exalted, and every hill and mountain shall be made low, the rough places will be made plain, and the crooked places will be made straight, and the glory of the Lord shall be revealed, and all flesh shall see it together....
>
> When we allow freedom to ring, when we let it ring from every village and every hamlet, from every state and every city, we will be able to speed up that day when all of God's children, black men and white men, Jews and Gentiles, Protestants and Catholics, will be able to join hands and sing in the words of the old Negro spiritual: "Free at last! Free at last! Thank God Almighty, we are free at last!"
> —Dr. Martin Luther King Jr.

Imagine. Three decades after his death, Dr. King's dream—at the time that's all it was—is still impacting lives. His dream continues to change how we see each other, who we sit with at dinner, what we hope for, what we're willing to die for.

> Imagine one man
> with one dream.

One man with one God-given dream.

What if God gave you such a dream, such a Chazown? What if your life continued to change the world even after you died?

Imagine one God-come-to-earth man with one dream. Two thousand years after Jesus' death and resurrection, the world is still reeling from the shock of grace. We still stagger at the gift of endless life, of absolute forgiveness, of salvation—undeserved, unasked for, unpaid for, freely given. What Jesus accomplished by living out the Father's vision for His life is beyond words. And yet so simple, so perfectly clear.

Listen to what Jesus Himself said about His purpose:

"The Son of Man came to seek and to save what was lost" (Luke 19:10). *Don't distract Me with anything else.*

"No one takes [my life] from me, but I lay it down of my own accord.... This command I received from my Father" (John 10:18). *He, and He alone, determines My life purpose.*

"I have come that they may have life, and have it to the full" (John 10:10). *My purpose is crystal clear.*

You'd have to agree—Jesus understood God's Chazown, for which He was sent. He could have quit at any time. Everyone else would have.

Yet He never turned aside. Never turned back.

Never.

Imagine. One disciple with one dream. The apostle Paul wasn't the Son of God. He wasn't perfect. (I think he wasn't even likable some of the time.) But he had the same kind of clarity about his purpose.

> What if your life continued to change the world even after you died?

"I consider my life worth nothing to me, if only I may finish the race and complete the task the Lord Jesus has given me—the task of testifying to the gospel of God's grace" (Acts 20:24).

Imagine one disciple. Imagine you.

What is your purpose on this earth?

What has God designed you uniquely to do?

When you get a vision for what God has in mind for your life, things change. A lot.

FOUR GIFTS

The first thing that will happen is that the vision God gives you will bring *focus* to your life. You'll know exactly what you're here to do.

When you begin to understand what you're supposed to do, you can better discern what you're *not* supposed to do. And this is important, because other people also have plans for your life. I can't count the number of *good* opportunities and invitations I receive from people. But *good* opportunities shouldn't distract from the *better* and the *great*. And because of the focus of my vision, I say respectfully over and over again, "I'm sorry. I just don't do that because that's not in line with the vision that God has given me."

The same is true for you. Every day you will have many opportunities to be distracted with "good" things. Chazown gives you the ability to say no to good things and say yes to great things.

With Chazown also comes *endurance.* God's plan is certain to include some tough times. Jesus assured us, "In this world you will have trouble" (John 16:33).

My wife, Amy, has given birth to six kids, with several pregnancies requiring extended bed rest. And every time, I am amazed that she is able to endure it. I don't know of one lady who thinks, *I'd like to gain thirty pounds. My body parts aren't big enough. Let's make some of them bigger. And I definitely want varicose veins and a bad case of gas. And at the end, I want to know what it feels like to push a cantaloupe through a garden hose!*

But when I ask Amy how she does it, she answers, "Craig, it's the picture I have of holding that little baby when it's all over."

With Chazown comes *peace.* How many people do you know who are wracked with anxiety over their identity, their purpose, their significance? With vision, when you wake up you know who you are and why you're here.

Several months ago, I was going to officiate a wedding for some friends. Their wedding was at a house that I had never visited. Although Amy and I left with time to spare, it wasn't until we were midway there that I realized I had left the map at home. Because the wedding was close to starting, everyone had turned off their cell phones. I had no way to contact anyone and no map to find the house. I was lost.

Oh, did I mention that my anxiety level was pegged at a ten? The right map would have brought me complete peace.

The same is true for you. If you are living your Chazown, you will live in peace. You will know that you are making the proper turns in life at the proper times to end up at the desired destination. (About the wedding: Eventually we stumbled upon the house by accident, very late and very embarrassed. In time, though, to pronounce them man and wife. At least they'll have a good story to pass down to their kids.)

Finally, with Chazown comes *passion*. You show me a person who has no motivation in life, and I'll show you a person who has no vision. Every single time.

All great people are filled with great passion.

Years ago, several British ministers asked the famous nineteenth-century evangelist D. L. Moody why his ministry was so effective. This was a fair question. You see, Moody would have been considered poorly educated at best.

Moody took the ministers to his hotel window and asked the men to tell him what they saw. As they gazed at a city park, all agreed they saw people. People in a park.

With tears in his eyes, the great evangelist said, "But I see countless souls who will one day spend eternity in hell if they do not find their Savior."[2]

This man had a vision to tell the world about Christ. His vision resulted in unstoppable passion.

And you've been blessed with a Chazown that can do the same for you. It's a different way to see your life.

IN THE PAGES AHEAD

In the pages ahead I think you'll find an unusual reading experience. (When we're talking about a human life and what it's really worth, "usual" would be inexcusable.)

We'll begin with the end in mind: writing your epitaph. Next we'll look at some surprising case studies of visionaries in the Bible. Then we'll search for your vision in three critical and very revealing areas of your life. These areas, which we'll represent as circles, are like personal Rorschach tests—you look at them long enough and prayerfully enough, and they'll show you important clues to your God-given destiny.

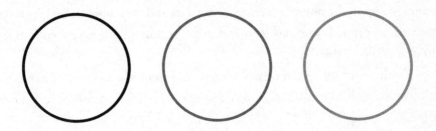

From there I'll help you not only find your own Chazown, but put it into writing. And not just the essence of your Chazown, but what you will need to accomplish to make it a reality. By the time you're done, you'll even know the very next thing you need to do to get things started.

> Trust me—His vision for your life is bigger and better than you've had the courage to even hope for. Your God is that good.

The last half of the book will help you succeed where many talented, motivated dreamers fail—in the personal disciplines, the small *c* chazowns, that are absolutely essential for a full, God-honoring, and rewarding life.

At various points during the discussion, you'll be directed to write in a journal. Use it to record what you discover and what you're still thinking through, and to plot your plans with God's help for a new kind of life.

Visit www.chazown.com for many resources that will enrich your learning experience.

If you read this book honestly, humbly, and prayerfully, I promise that your life will change dramatically for the better. That's what God wants for you. He eagerly waits for you to experience His amazing vision for you.

Are you willing to let God disturb you with dreams so big that you don't know how they'll be accomplished?

Trust me—His vision for your life is bigger and better than you've had the courage to even hope for. Your God is that good. That strong. And He loves you that much.

"DISTURB US, LORD..."

Sir Francis Drake once prayed a prayer that was later quoted by a missionary named Jeanie Curryer in one of her prayer letters. This prayer has changed my life. It went:

> Disturb us, Lord, when we are too well pleased with ourselves.
> When our dreams have come true because we dreamed too little,
> when we arrive safely because we have sailed too close to the shore.
> Disturb us, Lord.[3]

Are you willing to let God disturb you with dreams so big that you don't know how they'll be accomplished? A vision that can only come true if He pulls it off?

That's what you'll get if you come on this journey. If you seek God's unique life purpose for you.

> Are you willing to let God disturb you with dreams so big that you don't know how they'll be accomplished?

I won't promise the road will be smooth. But I do promise you can start today living with a vision for fulfillment. You will wake up every day with purpose and passion, motivated anew to fulfill your destiny.

No more wandering. No more emptiness. No more searching.

You will say, "This is why I was created. This is the meaning for my existence."

And God will smile.

YOU'RE THE AUTHOR

Plan Your Epitaph

Take a moment and write your final chapter, the way you want it to be. And as you do, think about your life *from this point forward*. Forget the past, because you can't change it. During those final days, how do you *want* to be able to finish the following statements?

Your Epitaph:

- The thing that was most important to me was…
- People say I stood for…
- I made a difference in my world by…
- God was glorified because I…
- People knew I loved them because…
- The reason I expect God to say "well done" is…

For more resources, visit www.chazown.com.

PART 2

CIRCLING THE TRUTH

Where to look for your own Chazown

3

DISCOVERING
YOUR PERSONAL VISION

A lot of people have narrow ideas about the way God conveys vision. Some expect to see writing—really big writing—on some wall somewhere. Maybe on a billboard beside the road.

Others are waiting for the audible voice, Drano-man style, saying, "Here is My vision for your life." (Hear the echo?)

And for those who prefer the King James Version, the voice should say, "Harken unto the Lord thy God who speaketh unto thee."

Yes, God used each of these methods. But not for everyone. Remember, God speaks in different ways to different people. Let's examine three examples in the Bible.

God gave Joseph his Chazown by means of a dream. The next day, Joseph told his brothers what he dreamed: "We were binding sheaves of grain out in the field when suddenly my sheaf rose and stood upright, while your sheaves gathered around mine and bowed down to it" (Genesis 37:7). Joseph had a vision or a dream that God's plan was to make him a great leader. And God did.

Moses, on the other hand, received his vision from God's audible voice, coming from a burning bush (see Exodus 3). As Moses bowed in the presence of God, the Lord revealed his life's purpose: to rescue the Israelites from Egypt, to lead them, and to convey God's word to mankind. And Moses did.

How did Nehemiah receive a Chazown from God? At the end of Israel's seventy years of exile, he got permission to return to Jerusalem. He discovered his vision when he looked at the destroyed city walls and he wondered, *Why won't someone do something about these walls?* (See Nehemiah 2:11–17.)

His vision came from a burden, something that bothered him, something that wasn't the way it was supposed to be. And Nehemiah devoted his life to solving the problem.

Each of these men perceived God's plan in his own unique way. And each one followed God's Chazown. That's why their lives made such an enormous difference.

How could God show you His Chazown for you?

Any way and any time He pleases!

Dr. Dennis Dunham, a good friend of mine, is an international recruiter for a private university. Although very successful in his career, Dr. Dunham expressed that something was missing in his life.

During one of his international business trips, Dr. Dunham visited an impoverished orphanage in Togo, Africa. What he experienced changed him forever.

Dr. Dunham discovered his Chazown. God was going to use him to help transform that orphanage—not just to feed them, but to educate every child and give them an otherwise unreachable life opportunity.

> God speaks in different ways to different people.

After eighteen months of behind-the-scenes work, Dr. Dunham raised enough awareness and interest to help build an orphanage, train Togo locals to run a profitable business, and feed children who would otherwise have starved to death. The children in Togo know of the American who has worked to change their lives. Dr. Dunham tells them he does it because Jesus loves them. He says it is his reason for living!

Is something missing from your life? Are you aware that God has more for you?

Seek Him. Just like Joseph, Moses, and Dr. Dunham, He will give you a Chazown. And not just any, but one that is tailored specifically for you.

Then you will know how you can impact the world.

4

UNIVERSITY OF CHAZOWN

As God gives you a vision, He will do two other things as well. First, He will start to work *in* you. "It is God who works *in you* to will and to act according to his good purpose" (Philippians 2:13).

Look at the life of Joseph. One step forward. Two steps back.

First, God gave him a vision for leadership. A miraculous dream. The next thing you know, his jealous brothers beat him, dropped him into a pit, then sold him into slavery. Surely he was crying out, *God, what are You doing?*

Then Joseph got a peach of a job. He was in charge of the mansion for one of the "suits" in Egyptian government. But even though he was completely faithful, he was falsely accused of rape, cuffed, and sent to prison. Again, Joseph must have lamented, *God, what are You thinking?*

> I've spent my share of time attending HU—Humble University. One of these days I hope to graduate.

Have you ever felt that way? Just when you thought you were on the right track—Boom! A major setback.

But God was working in Joseph toward a specific end. He sent Joseph to PU—Prison University—where he had to learn something that wasn't offered in any other curriculum.[4]

God often works that way. He sends you where you don't want to go to learn what you thought you already knew. I've spent my share of time attending HU—Humble University. One of these days I hope to graduate.

I entered HU in my early twenties while serving as associate pastor. I was thankful to be in ministry, but I had a burning vision to start a different kind of church. Like Joseph, I had my own question: *God, why can't I start my own ministry right now?* I thought my life was on hold.

But I was in school. God knew I needed to pass Humility 101.

One week my senior pastor asked me to lead communion Sunday while he was out of town. *At last!* my pride shouted. *My chance to shine!*

That Sunday morning, I stood before the whole congregation. Boasting my best suit and tie, I solemnly held the bread in my hands and recited, "This is My body which is broken for you," and then instructed, "Take and eat the body of Christ."

All eyes were fixed on me as I led by example, putting a piece of bread in my mouth. Unfortunately the piece was just a little too big. I tried gracefully to get it down, but I started to choke. Then to gag.

It wouldn't have been nearly as embarrassing if my microphone hadn't picked up every disgusting retch. Everyone in the congregation watched me trying not to regurgitate the body of Christ.

With only one liquid in reach, I veritably dove for the communion cup and washed down the bread, giving new meaning to the phrase "saved by the blood."

I still had more to learn.

When God gives you a vision, He will start to work *in* you. And He'll keep working in you until you've learned His lessons.

5

GRADUATION DAY

The second thing God will do as He gives you a vision is to work *through* you to fulfill the vision.

That's when it gets fun.

On graduation day at PU, Joseph didn't know that he had just earned his master's degree. He thought it was another day for staring at walls.

Meanwhile, back at the palace, Pharaoh was telling his chief butler, "I've been having these tripped-out dreams, and I don't know what they mean."

Now, it happened that the chief butler's alma mater was also PU, and he had been right next to Joseph in one of their classes. God had helped Joseph interpret one of the butler's dreams, and the prediction proved true!

So the chief butler told Pharaoh, "I know just the guy who can help."

Suddenly, Joseph was yanked out of prison, cleaned up, and brought to stand before Pharaoh. God helped him interpret the dreams, and Joseph was made second-in-command over the entire empire! In fact, God used him to save thousands and thousands of lives.

Imagine that! What Joseph desired least, he needed most. Only then did the phenomenal results begin.

As events unfolded, Joseph's brothers ended up standing before him, saying, "We're sorry. We're sorry. We're sorry."

But Joseph answered: "You intended to harm me, but God intended it for good to accomplish what is now being done, the saving of many lives" (Genesis 50:20).

Joseph was able to look back and see that God's work in him had to be accomplished before God could work through him and fulfill his vision.[5]

Setbacks are often setups for God to act.

When you seek God and He gives you your Chazown, He will also start working *in* you, so that you'll be ready when the time comes for Him to work *through* you.

God can show you His Chazown and bring it to reality in your life in *any way* and at *any time* He pleases. After all, He's an amazing God!

But the longer answer? The one to the question: *But what can I actively and prayerfully do to seek and find God's Chazown for my life?*

> Setbacks are often setups for God to act.

That's what we'll examine in the next section of this book.

I recommend a simple approach that's proven helpful in thousands of lives, including my own. Begin your search by looking carefully in three areas of your life. These areas reveal a great deal about the real you, and about the destiny God had in mind when He made you.

For our purposes, we'll call them the Three Circles.

CORE VALUES   SPIRITUAL GIFTS   PAST EXPERIENCES

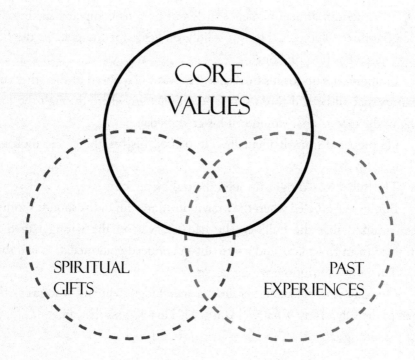

CORE
VALUES

SPIRITUAL
GIFTS

PAST
EXPERIENCES

6

HITTING THE RIGHT TARGET

An American athlete named Matthew Emmons competed in the 2004 Summer Olympics. He was solidly on track for the gold in the fifty-meter three-position rifle final.

Emmons was up for his final shot. He was so far ahead of the other competitors that all he had to do was send a bullet anywhere through the inner ring of the target. That would seal his gold medal.

He prepared himself mentally. He paused his breathing. He took aim. Then he fired.

The bullet passed right through the bull's-eye.

But he was puzzled when the tone indicating a hit didn't sound. Emmons then realized that the bull's-eye he had hit was on the wrong target. He dropped from first place, and a virtually guaranteed gold medal, to eighth.

The right shot hit the wrong target.

One day you will stand before a greater Judge than any who ever officiated at the Olympics. What will you say if He tells you that, in your life, you hit the wrong target?

You've probably noticed, though—we don't pay much attention to little daily decisions: who to talk to, what to buy, how to spend our leisure time, what deserves hard work, what needs to be let go. If these minor, moment-by-moment "bullets" of life are aimed at the wrong targets, we're not too worried. Truth is, we're probably not aiming at *anything* but getting through the day.

But stop and think. What is a lifetime? It's a whole pile of years and days and minutes taken up with moment-by-moment bullets aimed...somewhere.

What happens when enough time is filled with poorly aimed little decisions? Before you know it, a lifetime has come and gone, and you're startled to discover that you've completely missed the mark.

How do you guide those small decisions in such a way that they eventually add up to a life that's solidly on target? For that matter, how do you know what's driving your decisions every moment, whether you're aware of it or not?

You need to understand the first of the Three Circles that ultimately point toward your Chazown: core values.

K EY THOUGHT
What you cherish at your core is what you aim at with your life.

When God made you, He planted within your heart certain things you value deeply. They're hardwired into your heart. They're the values that, if you were to follow the path God has for you, would become the driving forces of your life. They're the things you'd be willing to die for. They explain how you come by your personal priorities.

Call these your *core values*.

Some common core values come to mind: the need for security, a love of adventure, loyalty to home and family, a passion for justice and fair play, pleasure in caring for others.

Whatever they are, your core values to you are like the pearl to the merchant in Jesus' two-sentence story: "The kingdom of heaven is like a merchant looking for fine pearls. When he found one of great value, he went away and sold everything he had and bought it" (Matthew 13:45–46).

This guy had spent his life as a pearl merchant. And he had seen the very best. Or so he thought.

One day he was going about his business as usual when a pearl diver pulled him aside and whispered, "I have the most exquisite pearl in the world."

> They're the things you'd be willing to die for. They explain how you come by your personal priorities.

The merchant chuckled and thought, *That's what they all say.* To the diver he said, "Okay, son, let's see what you have."

The diver glanced around, then pulled the merchant further into the shadows of a nearby building. Slowly he pulled out a small bundle. He opened fold after fold of cloth, until shimmering before the merchant was, indeed, the most exquisite pearl in the world!

He gasped. Suddenly nothing else he owned mattered compared to that glowing white sphere. "Don't show that to anyone. I'll be back in three days, ready to pay whatever you ask."

The merchant quickly liquidated everything he owned. He sold his house, his furnishings, his flocks and herds, his baseball card collection, and all the rest of his pearls. Then, at great cost, he returned and took ownership of one pearl.

Just one. But he valued that pearl above all else. And with his purchase, he had gained his heart's greatest desire.

When you are in touch with your God-given core values, that's exactly how you will think and live. Your core values will rearrange and direct your energies, your time, your thoughts. If you ignore them, sooner or later you'll be miserable. If you identify and pursue them, you'll unleash your potential and set yourself up for fulfillment and success.

What is most important in your life? Where do you refuse to bend?

Your answer is a core value. It's a driving desire or priority—perhaps different from that of anyone else you know—that God has placed inside of you to help you to know where to aim your life.

7

SPANNING THE VALUES SPECTRUM

Suppose I offered you a job just like the one you have right now. But it's in a state on the other side of the country.

And you'd make one hundred dollars more each month—a healthy twelve-hundred-dollar raise per year.

Would you take it?

If not, let me sweeten the offer. How about an extra thousand dollars a month? A twelve-thousand-dollar annual raise! Are you in?

If not, what if the raise were twenty-five thousand dollars per year?

And if that doesn't interest you, let me increase your current pay by *one hundred thousand dollars* a year. Would you take it now? (If you are thinking about holding out for more, forget it. This is my final offer.)

Your response to these questions provides insight into your core values.

Unless you hate your current location, you would probably decline the first offer. One hundred dollars a month is not likely to draw you away from your friends and local interests.

If the potential for more money doesn't grab your attention, perhaps it's because you value something else more.

I love my friends who are here, you might think.

My family is close by. I couldn't imagine leaving them for any amount of money.

My church is incredible. God is using me here. Why would I leave?

Perhaps you would decline all offers because you love your home. Or your neighbors. Or the climate. Or your local ministry to the poor. Or your favorite college football team.

Different people have different core values. Different life-driving priorities.

Take, for example, King David in the Old Testament. What might have been a core value for him? Well, he wrote poetry like Psalm 27:4: "One thing I ask of the LORD, this is what I seek: that I may dwell in the house of the LORD all the days of my life, to gaze upon the beauty of the LORD and to seek him in his temple." David highly valued *intimacy with God.*

And how about his son Solomon? I'd guess wisdom topped his list. Here's something he said: "Get wisdom, get understanding.... Do not forsake wisdom, and she will protect you; love her, and she will watch over you. Wisdom is supreme; therefore get wisdom. Though it cost all you have, get understanding" (Proverbs 4:5–7).

> What priorities make you turn down other highly attractive offers because you know what—for you—is indispensable?

How about some other well-known people? Mother Teresa? *Compassion for the poor.* Billy Graham? *Spreading the gospel.* Jane Goodall? *Chimpanzees.* John Madden? *Football.* Jack Bauer? *Nailing the bad guys.* Michael Scott? *That's what she said.* Well, you get the idea. What values drive you? What priorities make you turn down other highly attractive offers because you *know* what—for you—is indispensable?

8

WHY DO THEY DO IT?

Have you ever noticed how some people do things that seem very unusual to the rest of us? I'm not talking about weird stuff like snake handlers or obese men who wear Speedos on the beach. I mean people like:

- the businessman who serves breakfast to the poor every Saturday morning at six a.m. and can't figure out why everyone else isn't there doing the same thing
- the amateur naturalist (a mom by day) who can talk your head off for hours about the adaptive abilities of yellow spotted salamanders
- the busy teenager who mows the yard of the widow next door every week, then takes time to have tea with her on her porch…and wouldn't miss the experience
- the retiree who compiles and writes a two-volume history of Wide Spot, Wyoming, population 42

Why do they do it? How can these wonderfully different people do with such passion and joy something you couldn't *pay* a "normal" person to do?

The answer is simple: they value it!

Jerry and Annette are two such people.

One day, Jerry and his wife, Annette, visited our church. They fell in love with what God was doing and became very involved. Jerry had a successful career as a district manager for Target. His family lived a very comfortable lifestyle in a big, beautiful home.

When I invited Jerry to pray about joining our staff, he barely considered what his salary might be. His family prayed about it. They believed God was calling them to full-time ministry. And they said yes.

Because his salary as a pastor was less than one-third his Target salary, this family of five sold their house, and we built a two-room, thousand-square-foot metal building as their new home.

Why did they do it? Because one of their life-driving values is *serving others* empowered by another value, *sacrifice*. But get this—they define sacrifice as "giving up something that you love, for something you love even more." They know exactly what they're living for.

> Ken purchased seventy-eight T-shirts on sale, took them to a poor part of town, and just started handing them out.

I have another good friend who is wonderfully odd. His name is Ken, a roommate from my single days. Ken values *giving*. His whole life reflects this core value. He gives to the poor. He gives to the rich. It doesn't matter. He just loves to give.

At one high school state tennis tournament, Ken felt sad for those players who placed third or fourth and didn't receive trophies. So he tracked down all their names and addresses, bought them trophies, and delivered them personally to the players' homes.

Once, Ken purchased seventy-eight T-shirts on sale, took them to a poor part of town, and just started handing them out.

Another time, Ken bought a truckload of grapefruit (yes, a truckload). He picked a neighborhood, placed a box of grapefruits on each doorstep, and left.

These things seemed odd to me. Why did he do it? Ken valued giving.

What's unusual about you? What do you value?

Which leads to the practical question: how do you uncover your core values?

You may want to begin by identifying some biblical values that apply to everyone (yes, even extra-special people like you and me). Honesty, compassion, diligence, patience, humility—these moral virtues and many others aren't optional. They're God's way and they lead to God's best for everyone. For more on what the Bible has to say on these universally recognized virtues, read the book of Proverbs, Jesus' Sermon on the Mount, or the book of James. And remember: biblical values are not right because they're in the Bible; they're in the Bible because they're right and good and best...for everyone.

And now to the specific core values that define *you*. I suggest that first you pray and ask God to show you what they are.

If you don't know what to pray, try something like this:

> Dear God, I desperately want to honor You with my life.

Dear God, I desperately want to honor You with my life. You have placed core values in my heart to guide me toward Your Chazown for my life. Reveal those values to me. And give me the power to live by them. In Jesus' name, amen.

9

THE ANGER-BLISS FACTOR

As you prayerfully seek to clarify your values, ask yourself two questions that many other Chazown-seekers have found surprisingly revealing:

QUESTION 1: WHAT REALLY ANGERS ME?

We're not talking about your personal pet peeves. Like when someone near you in the theater talks through an entire movie. Or when an inattentive driver leaves on his turn signal for fifty miles. Neither are we talking about annoyances that trigger your temper tantrums because of sinful issues in your heart.

Rather, what stirs righteous anger inside you? What makes you mad on God's behalf? What offends your sense of justice and morality?

There were a couple of things that made Jesus angry. He once entered the temple in Jerusalem and found a bunch of merchants who had turned the place into a "worship emporium." They weren't interested in honoring God; all they wanted was a profit. So Jesus made a whip and drove them out.[6]

One of His core values, then, was the sanctity of worship.

Another time He got so fed up with the hypocrisy of the Jewish religious leaders that He chewed them out. If there was ever a time Jesus yelled Himself hoarse, this was it.[7]

So another of Jesus' core values was integrity.

I'll tell you one thing that makes me mad. I hate when Christ-followers become so self-focused that we think the church is only here for us. "What about *me*? What about *my* needs?" Sometimes Christians forget that *we* are the church, and *we're* here for the world.

I guess I'd say that one of my core values is outreach.

How about you?

If fake people make you crazy, then maybe authenticity is a core value for you.

If you can't stand halfheartedness, then maybe you thrive on excellence.

If rude people drive you up the wall, you might hold kindness or gentleness dear to your heart.

What makes you angry?

QUESTION 2: WHAT BRINGS ME BLISS?

I don't mean mindless, drug-induced euphoria. And I mean more than "I just *love* summer," or "Old movies make me so-o-o happy!"

Here's what I mean: What kind of relationship or activity brings you deep feelings of meaning and fulfillment, and happily drives you to achieve?

"God so loved the world that he gave his one and only Son, that whoever believes in him shall not perish but have eternal life" (John 3:16). God sacrificed His greatest Treasure for one of His core values—*you*.

> If you're exhilarated when guilty people get what they deserve, you value justice.

Jesus revealed what He took great pleasure in: spending time with outcasts, teaching, playing with kids, surprising friends, annoying Pharisees...

You might love helping people. Then serving could be a core value.

If you're exhilarated when guilty people get what they deserve, you value justice. (If you feel better when they *don't* get what they deserve, you're more motivated by mercy.)

If you're crazy about arranging flowers, beauty is probably a core value.

If you love cats, you have no core values at all. (Just kidding.)

What makes you angry? What brings you bliss?

These are the values that drive you every day of your life.

10

UNVERIFIED VALUES

Integrity is one of my core values. At least, that is what I have always claimed. For weeks, my wife had been asking me to get a state-of-the-art, high-tech, battery-operated baby swing for our baby, Rebecca (or Becca or Joy or RJ or JoJo—we couldn't decide what to call her). A new swing would cost seventy-nine dollars plus tax. My wife thought it was a bargain. Her tightwad husband was not convinced.

One day, I visited a garage sale, and lo and behold, there was a perfect used state-of-the-art, high-tech, battery-operated baby swing. They were asking only thirty dollars for it. *The Lord hath provided!*

I quickly shifted into negotiation mode. "I'll give you fifteen dollars for that swing," I told the lady in the driveway. She smiled and braced herself for some good old-fashioned bartering.

"Fifteen dollars?" she blurted. "It was a hundred new!" I knew it sold for seventy-nine dollars—plus tax. (Have I mentioned that?) The game was on.

I pointed out a scratch and told her I'd give her seventeen dollars, cold, hard cash.

She countered at twenty-five.

"Eighteen," I said.

She crossed her arms and squared her shoulders. "Twenty-three dollars and not a penny less."

Then I went for the jugular. I put on my pitiful, humble face. "Ma'am," I said meekly, "I'm a pastor with six kids. Could you give me a break? All I have is a twenty." Suddenly her countenance changed. "Sure!" she said, smiling. "Since you're a pastor, I'll give it to you for twenty dollars."

Victory!

I reached into my wallet while the lady watched. And discovered that all I had was a hundred-dollar bill.

Integrity was a value that I claimed but sometimes didn't practice. *Claimed* values. *Practiced* values. They aren't always the same.

I'm not alone on this. Peter claimed loyalty as a core value. He told Jesus he would die with Him. But a couple of hours later, when he had the chance to do it, he caved in and denied his Lord. He claimed one thing, but practiced another.[8] You probably know politicians, businesspeople, unlikable neighbors, and near and dear relatives who say one thing and do another.

And you? Put down your sweeping claims for a week or two and watch what you *do*. Do any of your claimed values differ from your practiced values? If so, at least you're in a position to get honest with yourself and make changes.

And you should. Because acting without integrity will end up hurting you.

KEY THOUGHT
*The difference between the truth that you know
and the truth that you live
equals the pain that you experience.*

If I could do it over again, I would rather pay seventy-nine dollars plus tax than go through the painful embarrassment and shame when my dishonesty was exposed.

God put a few passions in your heart. But as long as you deny them and live a lie, you can never live God's Chazown for your life. Only when what's inside lines up with what's outside can you hope to accomplish what He has called you to do.

> Put down your sweeping claims for a week or two and watch what you do.

11

VACILLATING VALUES

L iving with integrity is hard. The world tries to coerce you to adopt its values. Don't forget your spiritual Enemy loves to distract you from God's best. But we're citizens of heaven. God gives us the basis for our values.

If only we all truly believed that.

> If money were no object, what would you do for the rest of your life?

A few years ago, I experienced one of my most disturbing weeks in ministry. I surveyed about fifty Christians, asking two questions.

First, I asked, "If money were no object, what would you do for the rest of your life?"

I fully expected answers such as:

"I'd volunteer my time at the Crisis Pregnancy Center."

"I'd adopt children from a third-world country."

"I'd mentor young inner-city kids."

Sadly, the most common answers orbited around personal comfort. Instead of Spirit-led, selfless responses, virtually everyone gave answers like:

"I'd quit working, buy a nice car, a new house, a boat."

"I'd travel."

"I'd hire people to help me around the house."

Then I asked, "Besides ministering to your family, what do you believe is the number one, most important thing God wants to accomplish through you?" To their credit, the people were pretty honest. But I found their most common answer heartbreaking.

It was "I don't know."

How dismaying!

Do we really think God sent His Son so our greatest life goal would be a new boat? Do we think He created us uniquely and wonderfully, with all of our gifts and passions, so we wouldn't have to work another day in our lives? Or even worse, just so we would stumble around for years, ignorant of our reason for existence?

> We say one thing,
> but we do another.

And we wonder why we're so unfulfilled.

We say one thing—we want God's best, for example, or we don't want to waste our lives—but we do another.

What do you treasure? What do you stand for? What would you fight for? What do you *know* is so important that you'll let go of everything else in order to grasp it?

God has put your personal core values deep in your heart. They're there for a purpose, to help you aim for and hit the right target for your life.

It's time to know exactly what they are.

YOU'RE THE AUTHOR

Your Core Values

Let's get specific.

Keep asking God, "What values, what passions, did You place in me? What is the custom blueprint You engraved on my heart?"

As you pray, ask yourself, "What makes me angry with a righteous anger?" and "What do I absolutely love, more than anything else?"

Give yourself some time to think about these. When an idea comes to mind, write it down.

You can spread this exercise over several days or do it in a single sitting. When you've listed several possible values, narrow down to between five and ten core values, and then write them in your journal. You can visit www.chazown.com for help in formulating your core values.

For more help in uncovering your Core Values, visit the appendix at the back of the book.

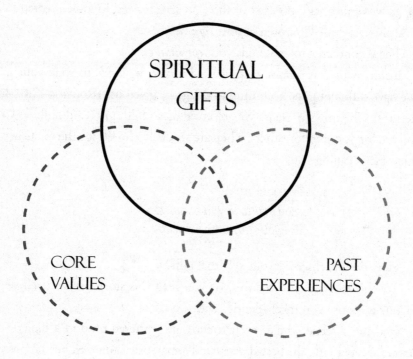

12

KEIRA, RED WITH PIE

As we've just read, the first of three areas you need to look at carefully to discover your Chazown is your *core values*.

The second area to explore is your *spiritual gifts*.

Just as your core values were planted in you by God, so were your gifts. "We have different gifts, according to the grace given us" (Romans 12:6). Unlike most Christmas presents you received as a child, gifts and abilities from God are for you *and* for others. They are specially chosen for the Chazown to which He is calling you.

KEY THOUGHT
God's gifts in you equip you for your gift to the world.

How do you discover your spiritual gifts?

Try this exercise. Just for fun. As you read this story, ask yourself which person's response you most identify with.

Imagine a scene where seven friends are gathered around a table to eat cherry pie. As Keira, the best-dressed and apparently hungriest person present, lifts a juicy red slice of pie to her plate, it somehow falls facedown onto her lap. What a mess!

> Keira, the best-dressed and apparently hungriest person present, lifts a juicy red slice of pie to her plate.

How each friend responds reveals their gifting.

Friend One takes charge, reeling off orders and organizing an efficient cleanup crew. She has the gift of administration.

Friend Two immediately makes an offer: "Keira, honey, I'll buy you another one! For that matter, another slice of cherry pie for everyone, my treat." He seems to have the gift of giving.

Friend Three leans back and states calmly, "I could have told you that was going to happen." He might have the gift of prophecy (though not of sensitivity right now).

Friend Four has already burst into tears, not because her pie or her dress are ruined, but on Keira's behalf. Four must have the gift of mercy.

Friend Five on the other hand shocks everyone when she laughs, then drops a slice of pie into her own lap! Soon everyone else is laughing too—and the focus is definitely off the first unfortunate friend. Friend Five was highly motivated to help her pie-stained friend feel better. She definitely has the gift of encouragement.

> There was only one event around that table, but there were seven very different responses. Which friend are you in the story?

After a minute, Friend Six gets everyone's attention.

"There is a better way to eat cherry pie," he says. "I've researched it. The first of nine things you need to know is…" I think Six has the gift of teaching.

And finally, Friend Seven. He has already completed a task without being asked—he has cleaned everything up. Seven is a born servant.

Now think for a second. There was only one event around that table, but there were seven very different responses. *Which friend are you in the story? Which response felt most natural for you?*

You are gifted by God. Knowing that, where do you excel? And please don't give me this false humility thing: "But, Craig, I'm really not good at anything." Just quit your whining, okay? (Perhaps God has *not* given me mercy.)

Be honest. What are you exceptionally good at? (Burping through the whole alphabet doesn't count. That's not a gift. That's disgusting.) When do people tell you, "You're so good at that, it makes me sick. I wish I could do that"?

Can you sing or dance? Are you good at gardening? How are you with numbers? Or leadership? Can you cook? Do you love delegating? Do others open up to you easily? Are you funny? Can you repair anything that breaks?

Look at Moses. He led two million people on a forty-year nature hike. And Esther rescued the worldwide Jewish population from annihilation. Their gifts? Both had leadership oozing out of every pore in their bodies.

And Nehemiah. He organized a ragtag group to rebuild a city's walls *in fifty-two days!* I'd call that the gift of administration.

In the book of Acts, we find a lady named Dorcas who used her sewing to help people. She had the gift of service. God even raised her from the dead because He was so pleased with her heart. (And probably because He felt sorry for her being called Dorcas.)

The Bible has several lists of talents and abilities (for example, Romans 12:6–8; 1 Corinthians 12; Ephesians 4:11), but these are only samplings from a much longer, unwritten "list" of gifts that God has distributed throughout humanity.

And think about all the well-known examples today:

Jerry Seinfeld jokes.

Meryl Streep acts.

John Grisham writes.

LeBron James dunks.

Every gift and talent you have came directly from God for a purpose. And He wants you to use them to benefit the body of Christ and be a blessing to the world. In 1 Peter we read: "Each one should use whatever gift he has received to serve others, faithfully administering God's grace in its various forms. If anyone speaks, he should do it as one speaking the very words of God. If anyone serves, he should do it with the strength God provides, so that in all things God may be praised through Jesus Christ" (4:10–11).

What are the gifts God has given you?

13

DOING IS BELIEVING

As you seek a clearer understanding of your gifts, ask yourself three questions.

PASSION

The first question may seem too simple, but it's right on target: What do you absolutely love to do? For example, do you enjoy leading, serving, encouraging, helping, giving, making others happy, or offering advice?

What do you enjoy doing?

When my daughter Anna was six years old, she obviously had the gift of encouragement. And she enjoyed lifting others' spirits.

One time I officiated an intimate, backyard wedding for close friends. My wife came with me and brought Anna.

Everything went smoothly (which is rare for a wedding), and the couple's love for each other was obvious to all. The holy event ended with a shout from little Anna: "DADDY, YOU DID FANTASTIC!"

Everyone burst into laughter.

This excited six-year-old is passionate about encouraging. She loves to make others feel good about themselves. And when she does, it makes a difference in their lives.

IMPACT

Which leads us to a second question: What do you do that has a significant impact on others?

Maybe you are a great listener. After airing life's problems to you, your friends walk away feeling better.

Perhaps you know a lot about managing finances. And people regularly come to you to help them make good financial decisions. Deep down, you know you are making a difference.

Or maybe you can repair things that break. Whenever someone is in a bind, you find joy in helping get them out.

Your gifts may seem insignificant to you. But not to others. What do you often do that is a blessing to others?

Mike and Sarah remember their friends' special days. Anniversaries. Birthdays. Significant moments. And they always send a card with a short note. Often they're the only ones who acknowledge someone's special day. And everyone loves to be remembered. They have told me how this seems small and insignificant to them, but it is big and very significant to others. Mike and Sarah are making a difference.

> Your gifts may seem insignificant to you. But not to others. What do you often do that is a blessing to others?

God gave you gifts. You will enjoy using them while making a difference in the lives of others as well.

SECRET BELIEF

The third question could result in a life-changing answer: What do you secretly believe you can do but have never tried?

Be honest. And dream big.

Laura did. For years, this young mom believed she could start a home business. Laura is great at making stationery and has a good mind for marketing. After seeking God for her Chazown, she decided to attempt what others said was risky. She read some books, attended a seminar, and swung for the fence.

Two years later, she is turning away business. Now, her home business allows her to work from home, spend time with her child, and contribute financially. She knew she could do it. She had just never tried.

You won't know until you try.

One of my close friends is very successful in business. He is also very politically minded. Deep down, he believes he could make a difference in politics. Everyone around him believes in him. For years he has considered it. Yet to date, he has not tried. My friend believes in the core of his being that he can make a difference in politics. But here's an inescapable fact: he won't know until he tries.

> My friend believes in the core of his being that he can make a difference. But here's an inescapable fact: he won't know until he tries.

The best way to discover your gifting is to start doing something. If a particular ministry looks attractive to you, it's likely you're gifted in that area. And don't be afraid of trying something new.

If you think you could make a difference, maybe God is trying to tell you something. Give it a try.

What are you waiting for?

Visit www.chazown.com to take a free spiritual-gifts assessment.

14

USE IT OR LOSE IT

My wife and I were thrilled when we moved into our first home and discovered that it had a garbage disposal in the kitchen sink. Our excitement faded when we found that it didn't work. As newlyweds, we didn't have any spare money for repairs. So for three years all our food scraps went into the trash.

All the while, two feet below the disposal was a small L-shaped tool. Actually I had noticed it the day we moved in. I didn't know what it was, but it looked important, so I left it there.

One day we told a friend about our nonfunctioning disposal. He walked over, leaned under the sink, and reached for the mystery tool. He inserted it at the base of the disposal, gave it a couple of twists, and voilà! The contraption whirred to life.

Elapsed time: two minutes.

For three years we had everything we needed to grind up old food. We just didn't put what we had to use.

A couple of thousand years ago, when the closest thing to a garbage disposal had horns and hoofs, Jesus told a story about a master and three servants. One day the master went on a journey. He gave his servants some money to invest while he was gone. To the first servant, he gave five talents. (A "talent" was a large quantity of money. Think of it as a million-dollar stock certificate.) The second got two talents. And the third received one. Then the master left.

Full of faith, the first servant took a risk and invested his talents. His aggressive move paid off, and he doubled the master's principal.

The second guy did the same and doubled his two talents to four.

The third guy hesitated, considered his options, and decided to play it safe. He buried his talent.

When the master returned, he promoted the first two. The third guy did not fare so well. The master said to him, "You wicked, lazy servant!... You should have put my money on deposit with the bankers, so that when I returned I would have received it back with interest" (Matthew 25:26–27). He took that man's money away and gave it to the ten-talent guy.

Jesus finished with the story's moral: "For everyone who has will be given more, and he will have an abundance. Whoever does not have, even what he has will be taken from him" (verse 29).

What a surprising story! The first two servants used their gifts and opportunities—and received more. The third servant didn't use what the master had entrusted to him. So he lost even what he had.

You and I have an opportunity to make a difference for God in our own lives and in our world with the gifts He's generously given us. And the rewards for our efforts will be greater than we can imagine.

Do you see how this applies to the big idea of Chazown? The upside of identifying and acting on our spiritual gifts is spectacular. The downside is anything but.

What gifts do you have that you're not putting to use?

Recently, my wife, Amy, felt God cultivating a gift within her that had been dormant until that point. He was encouraging her to teach other women and share the wisdom He was giving her. She wasn't sure about it at first and felt tentative. But she realized that what she was learning wasn't hers to keep—it could be the L-shaped tool to fit their need. Now she has accepted several invitations to speak and is partnering with another woman in our church to write women's curriculum. She's experiencing the fulfillment that comes when we step beyond our comfort zone to make the most of the gifts God has given us.

> You and I have an opportunity to make a difference for God in our own lives and in our world with the gifts He's generously given us. And the rewards for our efforts will be greater than we can imagine.

What about you? Is it possible that for days or weeks or years, you have known or had a strong suspicion about something God gifted you and called you to do?

I wonder what's holding you back. Do you fear failure? Are you afraid of being uncomfortable? Do you hesitate at the thought of being stretched? Are you stuck in a fog of excuses or doubt or missing facts? *(What's that funny L-shaped tool for, anyway?)*

God has given each of us a Chazown along with the gifts and opportunities to help make it happen. Our job is to work hard to identify them, and then to use them.

YOU'RE THE AUTHOR

Your Spiritual Gifts

You're well on your way to discovering God's Chazown—His vision—for your life. You've already uncovered your core values, the first of three areas to pay special attention to if you want to discover your Chazown. Now let's look closely at your God-given gifts and abilities.

Be patient as you answer these questions. Don't go too quickly. Try to come up with as many responses as you can.

1. What do you have a **passion** to do and enjoy doing? Or, what do you suspect you *might* enjoy doing if you just looked into it a little more? (Consider jobs, hobbies, recreational activities, anything.)
2. What do you do that seems to have a significant **impact** on others?
3. What do you **secretly believe** you can do but have never tried?

One of the best ways to find your gifts is to get involved in various activities and find out what works for you. When you're ready, record some of your possible spiritual gifts in your journal, as well as one commitment to a specific service opportunity.

For additional help discovering your spiritual gifts, use the free spiritual-gift assessment that is available at www.chazown.com.

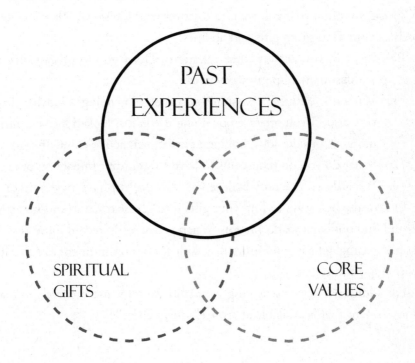

15

IT ALL HAPPENED FOR A REASON

The third promising area to explore to discover your Chazown is your *past experiences*. These are events or seasons in your life that God has given you to prepare you to fulfill His future vision.

God tells us in Romans 8:28, "We know that in all things God works for the good of those who love him, who have been called according to his purpose." The beautiful thing about "all things" is that it includes pretty much all things. The good things, the ordinary things, the not-so-good things, the truly (at the time) awful things. God has promised to use them all for good for those who love God and have responded to the call to live out their Chazown for His purposes.

K EY THOUGHT
*Your past often holds
the key to unlock your future.*

David was still a teenage shepherd boy when he faced Goliath. But already he'd had some valuable experiences that gave him the confidence and vision to take on the big guy. When all others—including the heavyweights in Israel's army—were saying "no way!" David reflected on his past. He remembered when a bear attacked his sheep, and God helped him kill it. Another time it was a lion, and God gave him strength to take it down.

Now, I assure you when David was looking that lion in the eye, he wasn't thinking, *Hey, this is great! I'm getting experience!* But later in life, his past gave him insight into his future. Standing with Israel's army, watching Goliath mock Israel's God, David said, "God has done it before. He'll do it again. Let me at him!"[9]

What might your past have prepared you to do that you couldn't—or wouldn't—do otherwise? Think about the positive experiences that have been formative in your life. Maybe a business success has given you the confidence to lead a nonprofit organization toward greater impact. Or maybe God healed you of cancer and now you are able to offer hope to others.

> What might your past have prepared you to do that you couldn't—or wouldn't—do otherwise?

Think also about the negative experiences that have shaped how you think, feel, and act. You suffered a miscarriage and never thought you'd feel happy again. But because of God's emotional healing, you now can comfort other couples whose dreams have died. Or your marriage fell apart, but because of what God has taught you, you now have the wisdom to help others in a relationship crisis.

My wife and I are close friends with a couple in our church, Mike and Diane. Diane is one of the most positive and godly women I know. She always sees the good in everything and loves to encourage others.

One day, Diane started to face some physical challenges. The once optimistic and fun Christ-follower sank quickly into a deep depression. She experienced repeated anxiety attacks and was paralyzed with dark, fearful thoughts. Overnight, everything changed for the worse.

Month after painful month passed.

Finally, through prayer, medicine, and the passage of time, Diane leveled out and once again became her jovial self.

She has described this often as an experience she wouldn't wish on anyone. But, surprisingly, she also says she wouldn't trade it for anything. On the other side of this painful memory, Diane has discovered a new dimension to her Chazown. Her life is now guided by a larger purpose. Any woman with depression is someone Diane wants to love. She seeks out those who are hurting and has devoted her life to counseling and helping them.

God works all things together for good. Diane will be the first to tell you that even bad experiences can lead to good.

16

MINING MEANING FROM THE PAST

H ave you ever found an old key and wondered, *What does this open?* I'll bet I have five or six of these mystery keys sitting in a bowl, together with a bunch of coins, paper clips, tiny screws, and a molar from one of my kids. I don't have a clue what the keys open, but I don't dare throw them away, just in case...

What if I told you that you have a bowl of keys sitting on a shelf in your heart? Not keys to start a car or open a padlock, but keys that could open windows of understanding to God's Chazown. These keys are your past experiences. Both good and bad. Those you look back upon fondly. Those you wish had never happened. And those—think about this—that you've never thought about seriously until now.

> There is purpose in your pain. Trust Him to reveal part of His Chazown for your life, even through your grief.

In order to mine meaning from your past, you need to examine experiences from both extremes. Buckle your seat belt. We'll start with the bad.

As we do, remember: God is good. He can use all things. There is purpose in your pain. Trust Him to reveal part of His Chazown for your life, even through your grief.

Ask yourself, *What painful experience might God want to use?*

I know, this is hard. We often want to ignore or forget the tough times. Even if you're afraid, you can open yourself to what God wants to show you.

Perhaps you had to file bankruptcy. You have a child who rebelled against everything you taught and stood for. You prayed for someone you loved desperately, and you believed they would be healed, but they died anyway. You were betrayed or rejected by someone you loved. You were abused. Or you were the betrayer, the abuser, and though you've done everything in your power to make amends, you'd give anything if it had never happened.

Take a moment and write down a few of your more painful experiences.

I hope the next step will be much easier: What good experiences have you had that God might want to use?

Make a list of some of the positive experiences God might want to use.

Think back to your childhood, and all the way up to the present. How did God bless you? Who impacted your life? Where did you succeed?

Make a list of some of the positive experiences God might want to use.

Great job! You've pulled up very important signposts that have been broken off and hiding in tall grass. We'll come back to take another look at these important responses in just a moment.

To discover how your past experiences help to shape your Chazown, visit Appendix A on page 227. There you will find resources that will walk you through creating your own personal time line.

17

EYES TO SEE

Did you ever see one of those "Magic Eye" pictures in the mall? You know, the unusual designs that, at first glance, don't look like anything in particular—just a random design. For years, people told me that if I looked just right, I could see three-dimensional objects jump off the page. After numerous attempts, I was convinced that everyone who said they could was lying.

Then one day it happened. I actually saw three-dimensional dolphins! I shouted out loud. Of course, that made me lose focus and I never saw them again.

But for a brief moment, I saw something I had not seen before.

The same thing can happen as you look back at the apparently meaningless collage of your past. Ask God to give you eyes to see the value in your experiences. Meaning and purpose have always been there, and God can help you see what you've never seen before.

I like the story someone told about a little bird. One day the bird was flying south for winter and got caught in a snowstorm. As snow landed on his tiny wings, it melted slightly, then quickly froze, causing the bird to fall to the ground. As he sat helpless and shivering, encased in ice, the bird thought to himself (to be spoken in a little bird voice), *This is the end.*

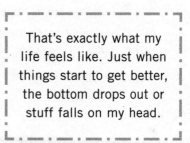

That's exactly what my life feels like. Just when things start to get better, the bottom drops out or stuff falls on my head.

To make matters worse, a cow wandered toward the freezing bird and—wouldn't you know it?—deposited a stinking pile of manure on top of the bird. (I know this is gross, but there is a point to it. Hang with me).

The bird panicked, horrified at the thought that he was going to freeze to death, covered in manure.

But slowly, the warmth of the manure caused the bird to thaw out. He fluttered his newly freed wings and began to chirp with joy!

"Chirp! Chirp! Chirp! Chirp!" he sang.

That's when a cat, drawn by the chirping, ran over, dug out the bird…and ate him.

Maybe you're reading this and you want to shout at me, "Craig! You're just too weird!"

I understand (but it's pretty much God's doing).

Or maybe you were reading along and you wanted to shout, "Yeah, Craig! That's exactly what my life feels like. Just when things start to get better, the bottom drops out or stuff falls on my head. My life is just one disaster after another."

I understand, and I hate when life feels that way. But God promises that He is at work in *all* things. Even the bad things. And if we will trust Him during the dark times, He can bring blessings out of the pain.

Do you believe me?

Well, back to that dearly departed bird. You see, this story of courage and calamity teaches three very important lessons. Hope you didn't miss them:

1. Not everyone who drops manure on you is your enemy.
2. Not everyone who digs you out of manure is your friend.
3. When you are in manure, keep your mouth shut.

Allow God to give you eyes to see His purpose in your experiences—all of them! It is there if you look closely enough. And when you see it, you'll find your experiences pointing the way to God's plan for your future.

YOU'RE THE AUTHOR

Your Past Experiences

We now have identified three important Circles or life areas that can help us identify and pursue God's unique and wonderful Chazown for our lives. The Three Circles are:

Our *core values*

Our *spiritual gifts*

Our *past experiences*

You're preparing to write the next chapter of your life. Its title might be one of these:

"Making a Difference"   "Taking the Faith Risk"

"Starting Over"   "Living the Dream"

"Restoring Brokenness"   "Shaping Up"

"Going for It"   "Close to God"

Now, in preparation for the next stage of understanding and living out your Chazown, explore these questions with me:

1. *What do your good and bad experiences have in common?* Look back over the experiences you reviewed a couple of chapters back. Do you see a common thread? Are they somehow related?

2. *What do you think your experiences have done within you to prepare you for the future?* How are you inwardly different because of what you have enjoyed or endured?

3. Now, regarding the next chapter of your life: *What possible title comes to mind when you think about the path ahead of you?*

For more resources, visit www.chazown.com.

PART 3

A DREAM IN DEED

How to name your Chazown and where to start

18

THREE-PART HARMONY

You're ready to answer the critical question: How do I discover God's Chazown for my life?

Look carefully at the Three Circles you've just identified for your life—your core values, your spiritual gifts, and your past experiences. By way of refresher...

- Your *core values* are the handful of values that you are most passionate about and stand for above all else.
- Your *spiritual gifts* are your special abilities, the things you do noticeably well—and love to do.
- Your *past experiences* are the events and seasons in your past (both pleasant and unpleasant) that have shaped who you are today and prepared you for God's plan for your future.

How do three such different areas relate to each other?

Are you ready?

Bring your Three Circles together, and find the place where they converge.

In almost every case, there's one identifiable "sweet spot" where these life-shaping arenas of our life experiences come together—the one place where all dimensions are at full strength!

Look where your circles overlap. That's where you find your Chazown.

God knew exactly what He was doing when He created you. God gave you core values, God gave you gifts, and God gave you experiences. And where those overlap is where His Chazown for your life explodes in spontaneous spiritual combustion.

> Bring your Three Circles together, and find the place where they converge.

God has a divine destination for your life. At that place where your core values, gifts, and experiences meet, what destiny do you see?

What dream has your Father placed inside of you?

In a minute, I'll help you get your Chazown down in writing. But right now, why don't you stop, take a deep breath, and try to say it out loud.

Finish this sentence: *"God has created me with a dream for my life, and I think it might be…"*

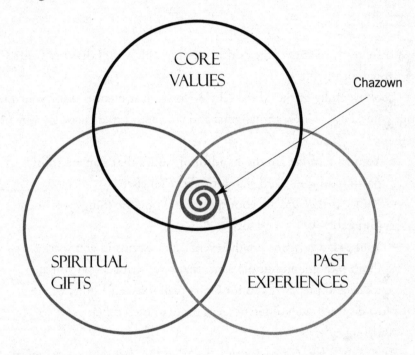

19

PERFECT FIT: A CASE STUDY

The first time I overlaid the three important spheres of my life—core values, spiritual gifts, past experiences—I was amazed at what I learned. When I do it now, I can see even more clearly the way those Three Circles in my life reveal important truths about my purpose. Out of the middle of that overlap explodes God's Chazown for me.

Allow me to use my life as a case study. Obviously, since I'm a full-time pastor, my story is very ministry based. But don't let that throw you—my motive here is simply to be as helpful as possible. Nothing I share is intended to be prideful or to tell you what your picture should show you. I'm just Craig— a flawed follower of Christ, a work in progress. But if you'll walk with me through this exercise, I can share with you what I've learned and what I see now about God's Chazown for my life.

First, what are my *core values*? What do I stand for? I would put six items on that list:

- Integrity
- Excellence
- Family
- Stewardship
- Generosity
- Evangelism

All of these burn within me, driving me to accomplish God's purpose for my life. You'll see in a minute how these tie in.

Second, what are the *spiritual gifts* God has planted in me? Leadership is one of the most obvious. Even as a young boy I was a leader—a junior fire marshal. (If you are ever with me in a burning building, trust me—I can get you out safely!)

Never underestimate a childhood passion. Mine for being fire marshal was a sign of things to come. All through my youth, God put me in leadership roles—captain of several sports teams, class president, graduation speaker, and president of my fraternity.

God has also given me the gift of evangelism. Talking to people about Christ makes some people uncomfortable. To me, it's second nature.

He also gave me the gift of administration. I love to organize, equip, and train people to release them to do God's perfect will.

Do you see a picture taking shape?

I'm most passionate about what I'm created and gifted to do. And so are you. Why would a loving God create you to do something well but not give you enormous fulfillment in doing it?

Third, what are my formative *past experiences*? When I was six, my parents hired a magician to perform a magic show for my birthday. Little did they know I would fall in love with magic (not the devil-worship kind; more the pull-a-rabbit-out-of-the-hat kind). Later, a neighbor moved in next door who "happened" to be a magician. He trained me, and by the time I was twelve, I was performing magic shows professionally. God used that experience to prepare me to stand in front of large crowds and keep everyone's attention.

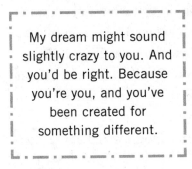

My dream might sound slightly crazy to you. And you'd be right. Because you're you, and you've been created for something different.

Another experience? When I was young, I found church to be the most boring, irrelevant place on planet Earth. Those endless hours left a taste in my mouth that now motivates me to do church differently.

How does all of this tie together? Where my core values, my gifts, and my experiences overlap, God ignited a fire that burned my Chazown, my vision, my dream into my very essence.

Now my sincere desire is to lead with integrity and excellence. I'm under accountability to stay in the race for the long run. I thrive in front of large groups, and I'm not afraid to take huge risks to get God's message across. I love to do church in innovative ways, and there are few reasonable ideas I won't entertain. I end up entertaining a lot of unreasonable ones too. (A magician knows there could be a rabbit in almost any hat!)

But the end result, I believe, is what my loving Creator had in mind when He imagined me. In both family and ministry, I'm doing everything in my power to lead people to become fully devoted followers of Jesus Christ.

God has given me a dream. I wake up every morning with that dream aching to burst out into reality.

I have a dream to redefine and empower the local church to take the gospel into the whole world. I have a dream to unite thousands of churches to make an impact around the world. I have a dream to train and mentor the next generation of leaders, starting with the six children directly under my care.

My dream might sound slightly crazy to you. Like it wouldn't quite fit your passions and values and gifts and past experiences. Like it wouldn't exactly get you out of bed every day with a jolt of enthusiasm.

And you'd be right. Because you're you, and you've been created for something different, fulfilling, eternally important…and unique to you.

But God's Chazown for Craig Groeschel fits me. Perfectly.

And yours will fit you.

Perfectly.

20

THE CHAZOWN COMMUNITY

There's not much in life that's more invigorating than working alongside other followers of Christ who want with all their heart to serve Him and know what it is He wants them to do. I call that a Chazown Community, and I enjoy being part of one every day of the week.

One person. One sentence. One very big Chazown.

Let me share with you just a few snapshots of the dreams God has given to my closest friends—the people I know and work with at LifeChurch.tv. Here are some of the vision statements that are changing lives in a big way:

> One person. One sentence. One very big Chazown.

"I have a dream to disciple a thousand women."

"I have a dream of being a part of God developing new and effective ways of planting churches in the twenty-first century."

"I have a dream to write a series of children's books to help make bedtime a lasting memory."

"I have a dream that our marriage would bring about generations of strong ministry-minded Christians who help change the world."

"I have a dream that involves reaching millions of youth and connecting their hearts with the heart of Christ to reach future generations."

"I have a dream for my children to marry godly spouses."

"I have a dream to give away over 100 million YouVersion online Bibles."

One person. One sentence. One very big Chazown. Whether they know it or not, every single person who is making a mark on this world for God today is living out his or her Chazown.

NAMING YOUR CHAZOWN

21

CLOSING IN ON YOUR CHAZOWN

From the first page of this book, I've asked you to begin dreaming, to open yourself to the Chazown God has for you. And we've been building since then toward the point where you will bring that dream into clearer focus.

When you look at that powerful place where the Three Circles of your life overlap, do possibilities immediately come to mind? If so, you're ready to begin describing your Chazown in such a way that you can remember it and live it. If not, keep looking, thinking, and praying:

What have I always cared a lot about? What values seem to define my very core?

What have I always seemed especially gifted to do?

What have my past experiences, both "good" and "bad," shown me about myself and my purpose in life?

God wants to show you something very important.

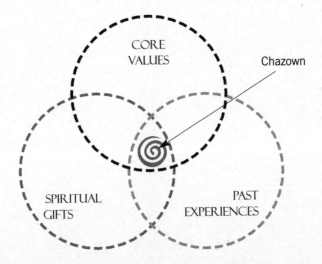

One exercise that I've found helpful is to wrestle with a couple of questions that I've already mentioned. These questions can be extremely helpful because they reveal our own hearts. And more—because they help us see past obstacles and obligations everyone feels but *that keep us blind for years to what God wants for us!*

> Ask God for guidance, and then start dreaming.

So take several minutes, ask God for guidance, and then start dreaming. Write your thoughts on a piece of paper, answering each question.

Question #1: If money were no object and I could do anything I wanted for the rest of my life, what would I do?

Question #2: Besides loving, caring for, and ministering to those who are most important to me, what is the number one thing that I believe God wants to accomplish through me?

You'll have more time to keep dreaming. (I hope you never stop!) But this has been an important next step, even if it made you very uncomfortable.

22

IMPOSSIBLE MISSION *POSSIBLE!*

Please understand one very important point: When God gives you a dream, you will be anything but comfortable. Why? Because...

KEY THOUGHT
God's vision for you is bigger than you can imagine and impossible for you to do on your own.

I call it a *God-sized vision*. God's vision for your life is such that when you see it, your first thought will be, *How can I possibly do this?*

The truth is *you can't*. God will call you to do something you can't do on your own, so you will have to take a step of faith into the unknown. The only way you'll accomplish it is to trust completely the heart and power of God. That way, when God accomplishes His purpose through you, God will get all the credit.

"Without faith it is impossible to please God" (Hebrews 11:6).

But perhaps what you feel is closer to sorrow than discomfort or fear. This is often the case when we begin to realize that we've been carelessly or purposefully disregarding what we know our Chazown to be. We feel that we have betrayed ourselves. We know we have disappointed God. So it's natural to grieve.

> God will call you to do something you can't do on your own.

But you can also take action. You can start bringing Him pleasure this moment. You won't understand all of the implications of your Chazown immediately. But keep your heart aimed toward His heart and purpose. With time you'll hit His target ever more accurately.

I guarantee that God's Chazown, when you and He fulfill it, will make a significant impact in this world, reshaping lives according to God's history-spanning plan.

So give yourself freedom to dream big! Let your dream overtake you. You were created one of a kind by God to show His love in a one-of-a-kind way to this world.

> Let your dream overtake you. You were created one of a kind by God to show His love in a one-of-a-kind way to this world.

And when you've dreamed as big as you can, dream bigger! If you have the ability to accomplish it without God, then it's not God's Chazown for you, and God won't get the glory for it.

By the way, if you run into a brick wall of doubt or confusion during this process, don't be surprised. It happens to almost everyone. Allow me to explain…

23

OF COURSE I KNOW WHERE I'M GOING!

The following is a mostly accurate dialogue I had with my wife, Amy, while pretending I wasn't lost.

Amy: *You don't know where you're going, do you?*

Me: *What do you mean? Of course I know where I'm going.*

(Silence.)

Amy: *No you don't.*

Me (gripping the steering wheel too tight): *Yes.* (Pausing for effect.) *I do.*

Amy: *You should have brought the map.*

Me: *You should have been ready to leave on time.* (Shouldn't have said that.)

Amy: *You don't have to be rude. Just pull over and ask for directions.*

Me (teetering between anger, embarrassment, and total frustration): *FINE!* (I slam on the brakes at fifty-five miles an hour and perform an illegal U-turn on a dime.)

All the children (eyes bulging, gripping any handholds within reach): *Aaaaaaaa!*

My seven-year-old daughter (after thirty long, awkward seconds of silence): *Daddy, you need to pull this car over right now so Mommy can give you a spanking!*

Are you like me—you refuse to ask for directions? It's dangerous enough to refuse help with directions on a trip. But that's exactly the self-sufficient "strategy" many people use in life. People who can't figure out where they are or where they're going *but are too prideful to ask for help* can end up just about anywhere. Or nowhere.

Look around. It happens all the time.

K EY THOUGHT
   If you don't know where you're going in life,
   put aside your pride—stop and ask.

The wisest man who ever lived said, "The way of a fool seems right to him, but a wise man listens to advice" (Proverbs 12:15). How about getting some good advice? Or asking for directions…from God *and* from the key people He's put in your life to help you?

When seeking good advice, make sure you go to the right sources. Just as an outdated map will mislead you, so will the wrong person.

Here are a few ways to seek and find godly counsel:

- Seek God's voice and direction through His Word. When seeking direction, I generally start in Proverbs. Many find great wisdom and direction through this very simple yet important book. You may find the help you need elsewhere in Scripture. Whatever you study, ask God to open your ears to hear His voice.

- Search for biblical advice from godly people in your church. Perhaps your small-group leader has insight. Or a person with whom you serve. Ask a choir member to pray for you. Or schedule an appointment with a pastor. Whatever you do, don't just talk about your struggle. Be quiet and listen.

- Look for those in the community with a proven track record. You may want to set an appointment with a business leader. Or a wise stay-at-home mom. Or someone with a great ministry or marriage. Or someone who has made tons of mistakes and learned from them. Perhaps you will read a great book or search for words of wisdom on the Internet. Don't limit yourself to seeking advice from those closest to you.

> A wise man
> listens to advice.

You may be very surprised who God uses to help direct you.

Seek help from godly people and great resources. But as I said, not every counselor can help you get from here to there in your quest, nor do they necessarily even want to. Some can even hurt.

24

GOD LOVES YOU

(and Everyone Else Has a Wonderful Plan for Your Life)

WARNING! Watch out for counterfeit Chazowns! Many other people—even well-intentioned friends—have visions for your time and resources, but those other visions are often inconsistent with God's purpose for you.

Peter once tried to talk Jesus out of going to His death. Jesus stuck to the plan. Peter's vision for Jesus was different from the Father's vision for Jesus.[10]

It is sad how often people surrender their Chazowns by ignoring God's direction and instead striving to please someone else.

My good friend—I'll call him Sam—came from a very wealthy family. Sam's dad loved Sam...and had a wonderful plan for his life: to carry on the family business. Sam's dad owned over two hundred very profitable car washes. And made a boatload of money. So once Sam finished college, his dad bought him several car washes. The stage was set for Sam to become megarich.

Only one problem. Sam didn't care about money. And he didn't like running car washes.

For seven long years, Sam lived a counterfeit Chazown. He hated it. Deep in his heart, he knew what he was created to do. Sam's values, gifts, and experiences all pointed toward coaching. Developing young student athletes was his passion.

Finally, against the advice of everyone (except his wife), Sam walked away from the big bucks, moved to a small town, and started coaching junior high boys.

He has never been more fulfilled.

One of my core values is family. Therefore my purpose involves spending a lot of time with my family.

Other people have their own plans for my life and time. *Come speak at this event. Have dinner with us. We need you on this important board.*

I say no a lot.

Some people understand, and some get mad. But I refuse to sacrifice God's Chazown for anyone else's.

You will have to do the same.

The world bombards you with counterfeit Chazowns. Businesses, advertisers, the Internet, every billboard you pass—all of them have visions for your money. But God's vision for your money is to invest it to bring the best eternal return.

Fast food restaurants have visions for you to supersize it (thus supersizing you). But God's vision for your health is that you eat well and take care of your body.

> I refuse to sacrifice God's Chazown for anyone else's.

Radio, television, and movies send moral signals telling you what is appropriate behavior. God's Chazown for your life involves a much higher moral standard.

Make it your passion to seek God's will and purpose for you twenty-four hours a day, three hundred sixty-five days a year for the rest of your life. That's how you will fulfill God's purpose for you.

And no one else's.

YOU'RE THE AUTHOR

Your Purpose Statement

Now I'm going to ask you to capture in words your Chazown, as you understand it now, in one action-focused sentence. Sound intimidating? It's not.
God brought you to this page for a reason. You're just a few simple steps away
from getting your life purpose statement into writing.

HOW TO WRITE A PURPOSE STATEMENT

*A purpose statement is simply a one-sentence version of God's Chazown for your
life expressed in words that greatly motivate you to pursue it for Him.* When you
write yours, simply say what action you most want to take or pursue with your
life, and what consequence you most want to accomplish with that action.
Look back at the Chazown Community, page 68, for some examples of exciting and very personal purpose statements.

A purpose statement isn't chiseled in marble—it's a working idea, a "this
is what is driving me today" version of the one big idea for your life as you understand it.

Think, Review, Pray

1. Go to your Chazown journal and remind yourself what you wrote
   down for the Three Circles. These key areas of your life are where
   God's fingerprints on your destiny often show most clearly. When
   you look at those areas together, what starts to become apparent
   about their overlap? What do they have in common? Toward what
   kinds of tasks or dreams might they collectively point?

2. Looking over your responses to these two questions from page 71
   might help guide you:

Question #1: If money were no object and you could do anything you wanted for the rest of your life, what would you do?

Question #2: Besides loving, caring for, and ministering to those who are most important to you, what is the number one thing that you believe God wants to accomplish through you?

3. What has God been showing you in the pages of this book? Ask Him to make it clear.

Write

Now write your purpose statement. Write it in your own words, in one long ramble if necessary. Then condense it into one sentence. Make it your prayer, your goal, your thanksgiving. And every day, ask God to bring it more into focus for you. He will.

1. My purpose statement in one long ramble (if necessary):

2. My purpose statement in one sentence:

Record

When you're ready, turn to your Chazown journal and record your thoughts as part of your Chazown purpose statement.

For more resources, visit www.chazown.com.

MOVING FROM
VISION TO ACTION

I have a dream...

25

MAKING IT UP AS I GO

Go back with me in time. I'm a young pastor, still in seminary, serving at a downtown church in a beautiful three-story building.

Very late one night, I was in my third-floor church office finishing a seminary assignment. Now it's some idiotically early hour of the morning, and I'm starting the hundred-mile drive to school.

Drive, drive, drive. Huge yawn. Drive, drive.

Suddenly I slam on my brakes. Speaking of idiots! That important paper I worked so hard on? It's still in my office.

> I'm standing on a ledge that is shrinking by the minute.

Three-point turn (legal this time). Drive (back), drive (back).

At 6:00 a.m., I find myself standing in the dark outside the church.

Unable to get to my paper.

Panicking.

Because I'm here so early, my magnetic pass card won't work.

If I don't get that paper, I'm in big trouble. Suddenly one of those light bulbs appears over my head. I remember that I always leave my window unlocked, because my office is three floors up and I know that no one is stupid enough to try climbing three stories up the outside of the building to get in.

A second light bulb pops up beside the first one.

Hey, my slow, caffeine-deprived brain says, *God has provided a way for me to get in.*

Spider-Man would be proud. Yes, that's right. I risk my life climbing to the third floor on the outside of the building. Why? Because I have a vision to start a church and change the world, but, well, at the moment my vision is in big trouble.

Climb, climb, climb. Grunt. Stretch way up. Climb, climb.

It's now 6:09 a.m. It's still dark. I'm standing on a two-foot-wide ledge twenty feet above the ground. I reach my window and give it a push. Then I push again. Chiding myself for not being able to open an unlocked window, I push even harder.

K EY THOUGHT
*When you fail to plan,
you plan to fail.*

No light bulbs appear this time, but suddenly my heart drops into my stomach. Someone has locked the window. I'm sure it was Satan himself, but I can't begin to guess who would have given him a pass card.

I'm standing on a ledge that is shrinking by the minute. I'm facing the building, clinging to the window frame, terrified even to turn around.

"Help," I whisper, daring a peek over my shoulder at the darkened street below.

Then again, a few decibels higher, "Help."

A ten-second pause.

That's when the terrified screaming starts. "Help! Help! Help!…"

Now it's 6:31 a.m., and the sun is starting to rise. Some random driver spots my backside poking out where a window should be. I flag him down. He tries to hide a grin while dialing 911.

Wait, wait, wait. Deep cleansing breaths. Wait, wait.

The time is now 6:46 a.m., and a fire truck is extending its huge ladder to me. With a fireman's help, I gingerly step across to the ladder and sheepishly climb to the safety of the ground. (I neglect to mention to the firemen that I was a junior fire marshal.)

I hug the earth. I'm in love with dirt and grass now.

When you go through life making it up as you go, trouble lurks just one light-bulb moment away. Guaranteed.

26

EVEN GOD
THINKS IT'S A GOOD IDEA

Would you please say that Key Thought aloud? "When you fail to plan" — (excellent intonation) — "you plan to fail."

Would you invest in a business that had no business plan?

Or board a plane with a pilot who didn't know the destination?

You'd never see a winning coach telling his players, "I want you to get out there and wing it. Wing it better than you've ever winged it before."

The scary thing is, most people improvise their way through life. And we wonder why we get stuck on third-story ledges without an escape route.

When you fail to plan, you plan to fail.

That's why we need God's Chazown for our lives. Once we have that clearly in mind, we need to take the next step — *a plan to make it start happening.*

Now, to some people, planning doesn't sound very spiritual. But God says, "Those who plan what is good find love and faithfulness. All hard work brings a profit, but mere talk leads only to poverty" (Proverbs 14:22–23). In God's opinion, not only is planning good, but implementing the plan is good too! "Mere talk leads only to poverty."

What's more, God Himself is a planner.

The Bible says in Psalm 33:11, "The plans of the LORD stand firm forever, the purposes of his heart through all generations."

If God plans, so should we.

Even Jesus set goals and implemented a plan: "From that time on Jesus began to explain to his disciples that he must go to Jerusalem and suffer many things…and that he must be killed and on the third day be raised to life" (Matthew 16:21).

And what did Jesus' carefully chosen and implemented plans achieve? The defeat of sin, death, and hell.

He overcame the grave. Not for Himself, but for us!

Jesus planned, and in doing so He planned *not* to fail.

A farmer plans, or he wastes his soil and his seed. A sailor plans, or the wind decides where the boat will go (on the rocks, anyone?). A businessperson plans, or the competition will win every time. Moms plan, or families sit down to eat around an empty table.

> We let circumstances and pressures and "necessities" just roll us down the sidewalk like a paper cup in a stiff breeze.

So why is it when we come to the most important priority of our lives—living out God's loving purpose for why we're on earth—we let circumstances and pressures and "necessities" just roll us down the sidewalk like a paper cup in a stiff breeze?

Fortunately, making and following a plan to realize your Chazown is as simple as, say, swallowing a moose…

HOW TO SWALLOW A MOOSE

How do you swallow a moose?

(One bite at a time.)

THE SECRET OF
LONG-DISTANCE DREAMING

Achieving your Chazown is a one-bite-at-a-time proposition. A one-step-at-a-time marathon.

Running a marathon is simple (I didn't say easy): you go down the road putting one foot in front of the other...until you cross the finish line.

How do you get from where you are now to the life-spanning Chazown God reveals for your future?

You get there one bite, one step at a time.

But you may be so exhausted from previous failures that you're wondering how you'll muster the energy for your next trip to the restroom. Perhaps you're frustrated. Disappointed. Maybe you'd love to have great relationships, but all you've experienced recently is conflict with those closest to you. How could you even hope those same relationships might turn around?

> You get there one bite,
> one step at a time.

KEY THOUGHT
*For long-term victories,
set short-term goals.*

God's dreams may seem out of reach in other areas of your life as well.

Remember the movie *What About Bob?* Bill Murray plays Bob, the patient of psychologist Dr. Leo Marvin (Richard Dreyfuss). What does Dr. Marvin tell Bob to do? That's right, take baby steps. And one little step after another, in ways Dr. Marvin never intended, Bob covers tremendous distances.

That's how God leads us to His Chazown. He knows exactly the pace at which we grow and learn. (He designed us, remember?) And He guides us by baby steps that lead us to His dream.

As you seek God, your best strategy is to set short-term goals so that He can give you long-term victories.

The path to every long-term victory in my life has been paved with dozens—maybe hundreds—of short-term goals. And the same will be true for you. Meaningful financial change is won by setting small, achievable objectives. Any success in a marriage rests on countless daily decisions (and a little chocolate here and there). Spiritual growth is a result of lots of minutes and hours seeking and obeying God.

> The only way to be sure God is the One guiding your steps is to "walk by the Spirit."

Of course, the only way to be sure God is the One guiding your steps—baby steps or giant steps—is to "walk by the Spirit, and you will not carry out the desire of the flesh" (Galatians 5:16, NASB). This means *not* making it up as you go, but consulting continually with God about every step.

As you learn to follow God's baby steps, keeping His vision for your life clearly in view, one day you'll look back and say, "Wow! How did God do so much *in* me? How did God do so much out in the world *through* me?"

He does it one step at a time.

What's His next step for you? Find it and take it.

Short-term goals help you realize long-term victories.

I have a dream…

Goal: _____

29

GAME-WINNING GOALS

If a purpose statement is a one-sentence description of *where* you're going and *why*, a goal is a description of *what you need to accomplish* to make your dream come true.

I'm going to ask you to set some goals. But before I do, let me clarify what makes a good and helpful goal.

First, a good goal is *specific*. Don't just say, "I'm going to get into great shape." That's a good idea, but it doesn't tell you what to do Tuesday morning at 6:30. Better to say, "I'm going to lose ten pounds." Or "I'm going to go from size 14 to size 10." Or, "I just want to jog a mile without dying."

And put a time frame on it. "I will lose ten pounds by May 31."

Second, a good goal is *attainable*. If I said, "I will be an opera singer by year's end," it's not going to happen. Main reason—I don't like opera. But even if I did, no amount of training would get me there. For me to sing well would require a miracle rivaling that of a resurrection.

If you have two car payments, credit card balances through the roof, first and second mortgages on your home, a student loan, and you've recently resorted to pawning your kids' Legos, an attainable goal is *not* "I'll be debt free by Friday." But you might be able to pay off one credit card in three months. How? That decision is up to you. Maybe you will stop eating out or cut cable television.

You can do it. If you keep your goals within reach.

And third, a good goal is *written*. Writing a goal is the first level of accountability. You would not believe the vast difference in outcomes that a written and an unwritten goal will produce.

I've read the following anecdote in a number of leadership books. The Yale graduating class of 1953 was surveyed to find how many students had written goals. Three percent. That's right, only three out of one hundred had put pen to paper.

Thirty years later, that same 3 percent had accumulated over 90 percent of the wealth of the entire graduating class.

That's the power of a written goal. Now turn that same power toward God's Chazown for your life. Just think what a few words in black and white can do.

YOU'RE THE AUTHOR

Your Short-Term Goals

It's time to write out your goals. Remember, a goal is your description of *what you need to accomplish* to make your Chazown a reality. A goal doesn't mean you don't expect and need God to act on your behalf; a goal is simply a written commitment of what you will do.

A goal doesn't lock you in or limit you. A goal sets you free from doubt. It defines your life's most important endeavors and motivates you to begin to make them happen. Don't worry if your goals change, or grow. If you're in motion, they should.

WRITE YOUR CHAZOWN PURPOSE STATEMENT.

See page 78. Record your personal life Chazown again in your journal.

WRITE YOUR SHORT-TERM GOALS TO HELP YOU REACH YOUR CHAZOWN.

Remember, goals that invite change are *specific* and *attainable.* Create as many goals as you want. When you're ready, turn to your Chazown journal and record your thoughts as part of "Your Short-Term Goals."

For more resources, visit www.chazown.com.

30

THE VERY NEXT STEP

A retired NFL offensive lineman says the toughest thing about staying in shape for a professional athlete is *walking through the front doors of the gym.* So that is what he focuses on. Getting in to the gym. Once he is there, good conditioning follows.

It's time to get to the gym. Or do whatever is the next step for you.

You have some goals. Congratulations. You are on the right track. But now that you have goals, what do you do next? It's time to take the next step.

Too many goals drown in a sea of good intentions. *I was going to get in shape. I was going to eat better. I was going to apologize. I was going to get life insurance. I was going to start a business. I was going to spend more time with my kids. I was going to commit my life to Christ.*

Your goals will begin to sink each day you don't act. Let's act now.

Ask yourself, what's the next thing I need to do to accomplish my goals? And by the next thing, I mean the very next step.

For example, if your goal is to start doing family devotions, your very next step may be to pick the night. Or tell your spouse. Or buy a devotional book. Or a DVD series. What is your next step?

> Too many goals drown in a sea of good intentions.

You might be hosting a big dinner party. And right now you are completely overwhelmed. How will you ever do it all? One step at a time. What is the very next step? Write your invitations? Pick the menu? Make your grocery list? Or call a caterer? Your dinner will be a success. One step at a time.

If you have a goal to get more involved in church, your very next step might be to sign up for a membership class. Or call to volunteer as a greeter.

Or set an appointment with a pastor. Or simply make a commitment to attend church this weekend. What is your next step?

Maybe you have a goal to present a new idea to

> Keep your goals
> rolling forward.

your boss. Your very next step might be to type out the idea. Or make a PowerPoint presentation. Or schedule an appointment. Or run the idea by three other people for their advice. Write down your next step.

Keep the wheel turning. Keep the ball moving. Keep the bike in motion.

An object moving forward gains momentum. An object at rest tends to stay at rest. Keep your goals rolling forward.

Your goal may at first seem too big or intimidating to tackle. You may freeze with a feeling of being overwhelmed. Many have analysis paralysis, not knowing how to achieve such a big goal.

Take the very next step.

I have a dream...

    Goal: _____

    The very next thing I'm going to do is _____

YOU'RE THE AUTHOR

Your Very Next Step

On page 90 you were directed to write short-term goals. Review the goals you wrote down. Now write out action steps for each goal in your Chazown journal.

1. The goal you will move toward is:
2. The very next step you are going to take to accomplish your goal is:
3. *How* you are going to accomplish the very next step:
4. *When* you will take the very next step:

For more resources, visit www.chazown.com.

PART 4

THE FIVE SPOKES
OF CHAZOWN

Where you need to succeed "small"

so you can succeed big

31

PICTURE THIS

Looking back, do you see your life differently? Before we take the next important step toward your future, let's review how far we've come in just a few pages:

It's been a long and exhilarating journey from the idea that something is waiting for you at the end of your life.

Beginning, then, with the end in mind, you agree with King David when he declared in Psalm 139:14: "I am fearfully and wonderfully made."

Far from being an accident, you are a lovingly created being—made to know God's custom-made, perfect vision for your life, and live it with your whole heart. Talk about good news! The Hebrew word for that powerful, one-of-a-kind, and very personal purpose is: Chazown.

Chazown means dream or revelation or vision. (Where there is no vision... well, you know what happens.) But for you, the news keeps getting better. Like Jesus, Paul, Martin Luther King Jr., and everyone who is making a difference for God, you have a Chazown. You have a dream.

"I have a dream..."

In this book, we've been picturing our Chazown as a spiral.

Everyone has a Chazown. Not everyone lives it. But you've chosen to find your Chazown and pursue it (like you were created to do). More good news (and a huge sigh of relief): God didn't mean for anyone to muddle around for years in the dark about their Chazown. He wants you to own your own Chazown—and He's promised to help.

For example, the clues to our personal Chazown are usually staring right at us if we look in three critical areas where God's been lovingly at work since the day we were born.

These areas are our core values, our spiritual gifts, and our past experiences:

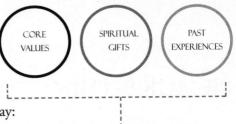

Then, what really helps is to put those circles together in an overlay:

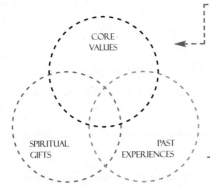

Shazam! I mean, *Chazown!* There it is—almost every time. Right where the Three Circles converge, God's vision for our future is ready to burst into view.

Anyone who gets their Chazown in sight should write it down—to remember it, pray it, live it—and you did. Your Chazown captured in a simple sentence and expressed in a way that greatly motivates you to pursue it is a vision or purpose statement.

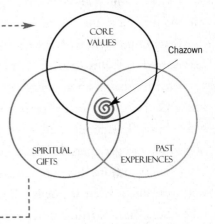

But to turn a vision into reality, you need a plan. You need to know which direction to go. That's where goals come in:

I have a dream… _____

Once you have your goals clearly in mind, there's only one thing left.

Begin. Take the very next step. And this is where the action (and the fun) really begins. I promise.

All you have to do is turn the page…

I have a dream… _____
  ❏ Goal: _____

❏ Goal: _____
  The very next thing
I'm going to do is… _____

32

SPEAKING OF SPOKES

Lance Armstrong is amazing on a bicycle. Somewhere along the line, his courage and determination grabbed my attention, and I started to follow the sport of cycling.

Before long I decided to give it a try. So I bought some funny-looking tight shorts with a padded bottom, the helmet, the shoes, and a used street bike. I was ready for my first eighty-mile ride. Twenty miles into it, I threw up on the side of the road.

I'm no Lance Armstrong.

But I am learning about cycling. And getting somewhat better. Now I can do a fifty-mile ride and keep from chunking my lunch.

Several months into my new sport, I learned something about my bike. On a short ride, one of the spokes on the wheel became loose. Within minutes, other spokes started to spring loose. In less than a mile of traveling and without warning, the whole bike became unstable. Moments later, I crashed.

> Why do so many gifted people self-destruct? Everything on the outside of their lives can look so good. But something unseen isn't right.

And it all started with one loose spoke.

Each spoke matters. When one is not in its proper place, the integrity of the whole wheel and bike is compromised. And eventually it stops working.

Stranded twenty miles from home on a broken bike, I saw a haunting parallel to life. People streak off for a win in life, something they thought was minor comes loose...and they end up wrecked.

What I'm about to tell you I have rarely talked about publicly. It has been too personal and painful.

My first mentor in ministry was a great man of God. His life was radically changed by the love of Jesus, and his passion for God and people was contagious. Hundreds of church members loved and respected his leadership. He knew his Chazown and was living it with intensity.

Then one day one of his spokes came loose.

He stopped praying. Then he stopped reading his Bible. Then he shied away from accountability.

More spokes came loose.

One day he met a girl that he liked. This girl was not his wife. And he crossed a line.

Multiple spokes sprung loose, causing his life to wobble dangerously.

An affair. Lies. Theft. Deceit. Cover-up. And more lies.

Then my trusted friend and mentor crashed.

And he never recovered.

Some years ago, my mentor and friend took his life, leaving a broken wife, two damaged children, and a severely wounded church.

You know similar stories. Maybe yours don't have such a dramatic ending. Rather than having a sudden end, the person you know may still be dying a slow and agonizing death. He may be alive physically but dying spiritually, relationally, and emotionally.

Why do so many gifted people self-destruct? Everything on the outside of their lives can look so good. But something unseen isn't right.

A spoke came loose.

One broken spoke led to another. Then another. They thought they were still riding a high-speed bike. Sure looked like it from the outside. But they were a crash waiting to happen.

Then one day it did.

I assure you, my mentor had as much promise to affect this world for God's glory as anyone I have ever known. Watching his life unravel was more painful than I can describe. I will be forever different because of his bad decisions.

With God's help I will not crash. Period.

You will never know the level of passion and truth that I've placed into those words. I will not crash.

I will *not* lose my marriage! I will *not* devastate my children! I will *not* damage the church! And I will *not* tarnish the name of Christ!

I will not crash!

Like the apostle Paul, I will "finish the race and complete the task the Lord Jesus has given me" (Acts 20:24).

And you can too. We can finish strong. If we keep the spokes tight.

KEY THOUGHT
Where there is no vision to follow Jesus fully, good dreams perish.

When we talk about a Chazown, a big dream, what exactly do we mean by the word *spoke*?

I'm using the image of spokes in the wheel of a racing bike to illustrate those sometimes-overlooked fundamentals or supporting priorities in our lives that must be fully devoted to God. If they're not, long-term success in achieving our Chazown is just not going to happen.

> We can finish strong. If we keep the spokes tight.

In my experience, there are five extremely important fundamentals or "spokes" to pay attention to in life. You could certainly name other spokes, but based on my experience, these keep proving to be the big ones:

- Your relationship with God
- Your relationships with people
- Your financial health
- Your physical health
- Your life's work

Each of these fundamentals must be in order for you to finish the race as you pursue living out your Chazown for God.

I'll use my life as an example.

I couldn't do ministry for long if my relationship with God suffered. Imagine if I drifted from God and started entertaining sin. Looking lustfully. Slipping into greed. Or depending on my own abilities rather than the power of God. What if I lost my love for the lost? Or put my name above the name of Christ? Without a growing relationship with God, my life and ministry would quickly wither and die.

What if I lacked integrity in relationships? What if I neglected my wife? Or avoided accountability? Or became bitter? Or hung out with the wrong people? Life, for me, would break down.

What if I preached freedom in Christ, but lived in the grip of materialism, then slid into the bondage of debt, then filed bankruptcy? What kind of witness would that make for the kingdom of God?

> Each of these fundamentals must be in order for you to finish the race as you pursue living out your Chazown for God.

Or what if I was grossly out of shape? Or dressed like a slob? Or lived with unchecked high blood pressure? My ability to influence others for Christ would be limited dramatically.

What if I was unsure of my call to full-time ministry? Always looking around at other careers, wondering if there was something better? Or stuck in some dead-end job when I knew I was called to something else? My effectiveness would be limited.

If any of the big five spokes became loose, I could look like I was successfully pursuing my destiny, but actually I'd be in trouble and heading for a wreck.

And so would you.

That is why we're going to pursue God's Chazown for these five important life priorities. Think of these fundamentals as chazown with a lowercase *c*. Why? Because God has a perfect best for you in each of these areas too—not just in the big picture of your destiny on earth. Fact is, you can't get to your destiny— your big *C* Chazown—without seeking God's best in the key supporting areas that make it possible.

It's time to be honest with ourselves. Let's get the small *c*'s right so we will finish strong. Let's pursue God fully, before we spin out and wreck our lives and the lives of others.

That's why I created this personal equation for life. Hundreds of my friends have committed to follow this equation and are living in the blessings of God's Chazown for their lives. The equation goes like this:

You surrender your life to God and His Chazown for you

+

You take care of the fundamentals (small *c* chazowns) He puts before you

+

You establish goals

+

You take the next step

+

You live with proper accountability

=

Your God-given destiny will take care of itself!

While the choice to pursue your Chazown is up to you, the real work of it is God's. It's His power at work in you (see 2 Corinthians 12:9). *Your* work is to be faithfully devoted to Him.

So in the next section of the book, we'll focus on the fundamentals (the small *c*'s) that support your big *C* Chazown.

Put on your helmet, your shoes, and those funny-looking shorts. Because we're going for a ride.

TOTAL SUCCESS

The purpose of any plan is success. For a Christian, success means becoming who God wants us to be. It helps me to make that statement even more personal: I define success as *being a fully devoted follower of Christ*.

As simple as that definition seems, it is based on two big assumptions. First, it involves not just arrival at the destination, but also the journey. Real success starts right now, and it continues every day you live on earth.

For instance, if one of your chazowns is business success, but on the way you hurt your family or behave dishonestly, then you haven't succeeded, even if you end up with greater wealth than Bill Gates.

If you set out for the destination of feeding homeless people but you don't deepen your relationship with God, you've missed the main point, and you've failed.

Success is determined by your day-to-day decisions on the way to your Chazown.

Wrestle with this question: When is a championship team successful? Is it only during the last seconds of the final game, when the crowd goes wild? No, that's just the destination. The team's true success began even before the first day of practice, when each player began building strength, stamina, and specialized skills. Every day that the team worked hard, learned to play together, listened to the coach, grew from mistakes, won a game, or lost a game—every step of that journey was part of that team's success.

Success is who you are today, not just who you are at the end of your life. Success is being a fully devoted follower of Christ right now.

The second assumption in my definition of success is wrapped up in the word *fully*. Notice the definition doesn't say success is being a *partially* devoted follower of Christ. Or a *when-it's-convenient* follower. Or *in this area but not that one.*

Success for a Christian is following Christ...*fully.*

That means every area of life belongs to Him.

Most of the rest of this book will help you develop an action plan with specific, achievable, written goals in the five fundamental life priorities I've already identified:

1. **Your relationship with God.** I'll help you move toward God's dream for your experience of life with Him. You'll discover what God wants you to do differently, in small steps starting now, in order to achieve His chazown in the most critical of all life's pursuits. God Himself.

2. **Your relationships with people.** How will you find satisfaction and accomplish the greatest impact as a friend, as a brother or sister, in marriage, as a parent or grandparent, as an employee, and in all of your various interpersonal connections? How are other believers encouraging you toward your Chazown? How are you helping them to achieve theirs?

3. **Your financial health.** Way too many Christians are seriously hindered from using their God-given wealth for eternity because of debt, poor spending habits, and poor investment decisions. You can start today, taking baby steps, to shift your financial bottom line toward God's incredible dreams, which extend far beyond any bank account or stock portfolio.

4. **Your physical health.** Since your body is the temple of the Holy Spirit,[11] how's your housekeeping for God going? Maybe you just need ongoing routine maintenance. Or maybe you need a major renovation. Together we can set up the blueprints for success.

5. **Your life's work.** Your work is whatever you do with your productive, waking hours, even if you don't get a paycheck for doing it. Are you pursuing the life tasks God has created you to accomplish? Are you just merely existing for a paycheck, or do you thrive at your work because you're fulfilling a dream? We'll think this through and, if necessary, determine course corrections for you.

YOU'RE THE AUTHOR

Self-Inventory in the Five Fundamentals

You have a couple of options for reading and writing the rest of your book.

Option #1: You can focus on *one* of the five key disciplines, go and live your action plan in that part of life for a while, then come back and create a plan for another area.

Option #2: You can work on action plans in all five (or two or four) fundamentals. If you do this, I still encourage you to implement only one plan at a time.

Either way, I've provided a survey to help you determine the areas where you might be most hungry for vision. Mark any of the following that are true for you:

YOUR RELATIONSHIP WITH GOD

- I usually feel distant from God.
- I don't spend much time praying or reading the Bible.
- I'm inconsistent in my relationship with God.
- I struggle with doubts about God.
- I am not involved in a church. (Attending only occasionally is not being involved.)

YOUR RELATIONSHIPS WITH PEOPLE

- I am in one or more painful or destructive relationships.
- I often feel lonely.
- In few (or none) of my relationships am I helping others draw closer to Christ, nor are they doing that for me.

- I do not have a mentor.
- I fear intimacy.

YOUR FINANCIAL LIFE

- I carry credit card balances from month to month.
- I feel financially hindered from doing some things God wants me to do.
- I'm often worried about finances.
- If I didn't have an income for one month, I couldn't pay my bills.
- I'm not tithing 10 percent of my income to God.

YOUR PHYSICAL HEALTH

- I'm often tired and worn down.
- I struggle with sexual promiscuity, smoking, or drug or alcohol abuse.
- I haven't had a physical in years.
- I don't exercise regularly.
- I think the four basic food groups are Taco Bell, McDonald's, Wendy's, and KFC.

YOUR LIFE'S WORK (INCLUDING VOLUNTEER SERVICE AND RAISING FAMILY)

- I feel little or no passion about my work.
- I dream about doing something different.
- I don't think my work has much, if anything, to do with God.
- My gifts and passions are underutilized.
- I don't have a clue what I need to do with this part of my life.

The categories in which you marked the most statements are the ones you might consider giving priority attention. But pray about your decision, and go the direction God wants you to go.

Option #1: If you want to start an action plan just for…

…your **relationship with God**, go to page 109.

...your **relationships with people**, go to page 123.

...your **financial life**, go to page 143.

...your **physical health**, go to page 163.

...your **life's work**, go to page 179.

Option #2: If you want to work on plans in **all five fundamentals**, then simply work through the rest of this book in sequence.

For more resources, visit www.chazown.com.

RELATIONSHIP WITH GOD

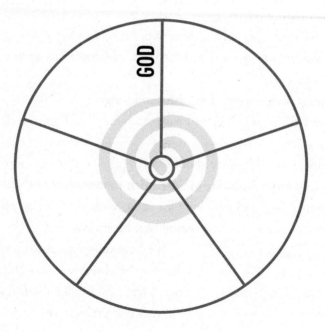

34

LIKE FISH NEED WATER

Y ou may wonder why a relationship with God is required for you to reach your Chazown. Some may argue: *Can't I just be a decent law-abiding person with good morals and enjoy the best of life? I know plenty of successful people who don't pay much, if any, attention to their spiritual life. So what's the big deal with the God-stuff, anyway?*

The God-stuff, your relationship with Him, is as big as any *stuff* can get. You and I were made by God and for God. He created us to know and love Him. We need God.

Like lungs need oxygen. Like fish need water.

"In him we live and move and have our being," said the apostle Paul (Acts 17:28).

The Bible is one big story about God in pursuit of man, and man in pursuit of God. From the first day in the garden to the coming of Christ and His eventual return, God came looking for us, to walk with us and talk to us. To know and be known.

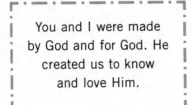

You and I were made by God and for God. He created us to know and love Him.

We have only one major problem. And it has hindered man's relationship with God since Adam and Eve ate the forbidden fruit. God calls our problem sin.

Whether we admit to it or not, we can't be complete or happy until we bring our greatest need to God and ask Him to meet it.

So yes, you can live a moral life and be better for it. You can live by the Bible and have a better life. But that would be like living by your parents' house rules as a child without receiving their love and giving them yours in return. You'd have a well-run house, but not a home. God created you for Himself. He made you to find your home in Him.

In the same way, your whole Chazown doesn't exist outside of a living, growing relationship with the One who made you. (If you would say that you have never come to God through Christ, don't spend another moment living at a distance from Him. Pursue Him. He is already pursuing you. For specific direction, turn to "Already Living with Regrets?" on page 215.)

> It won't happen by accident.

So how can you know and pursue God's chazown for your relationship with Him? Before we discover the answer, let me promise you something: it won't happen by accident.

35

THE ACCIDENTAL DISCIPLE

As a kid, I loved "Goldilocks and the Three Bears." While the bears were out, Goldilocks ate the bears' porridge. (Bears and porridge? I never understood that. And living in a house? Oh well.) Papa Bear's porridge was toooo hot and Momma Bear's toooo cold. But Baby Bear's was juuussst riigghht.

Not too hot. Not too cold.

Jesus is nothing like Goldilocks.

He said to a group of late first-century Christians, "You are neither cold nor hot. I wish you were either one or the other! So, because you are lukewarm—neither hot nor cold—I am about to spit you out of my mouth" (Revelation 3:15–16). Can you tell He's not happy?

KEY THOUGHT
Where there is no vision for our relationship with God, we tend to drift away from Him.

Everyone falls into one of three categories. You're either hot, cold, or lukewarm.

Hot means you're *growing in your relationship with God*. That's how Paul described the Christians in a Greek city called Thessalonica: "Your faith is growing more and more, and the love every one of you has for each other is increasing" (2 Thessalonians 1:3). Growing closer to God doesn't just mean more knowledge; it means your heart is expanding for God and for people. And as with any relationship, a growing relationship with God as a follower of Jesus Christ only happens on purpose.

There are no accidental disciples.

Cold people are those who *don't know God yet*. They don't have a relationship with Christ. The reason this category is not at the bottom of Jesus' list is that the cold person is not pretending, as is a Christian who turns away from God.

Lukewarm. This is the category Jesus found so tasteless that He couldn't stomach it. The lukewarm person is one who is *drifting*. You have a relationship with God, but the quality of the relationship is fading. Hebrews 2:1 warns, "We must pay more careful attention, therefore, to what we have heard, so that we do not drift away."

One summer day my family was at the beach. We were playing in the surf right in front of our cabin for an hour or so. But when I looked up for our beach cabin, it was four cabins away. I asked myself, *How did we get way over here?* Little by little, we had drifted. It happened so gradually I didn't notice until I looked up. Then my point of reference showed me we had moved a long way.

That's where many people are in their relationship with God. On the outside they may look like hot Christians, but inwardly their hearts have drifted.

God wants you hot.

Hot with passion to know Him intimately. Hot with desire to internalize His Word and love His people. Burning within to follow His voice. Aching in your heart for those who are lost. Full of righteous anger against sin.

> I asked myself, How did we get way over here? Little by little, we had drifted.

But maybe you suspect your heart for God has cooled to room temperature—the temperature of the environment around. If so, it's time for you to look up. Compare your situation now with your reference point—a white-hot relationship with God. Then get back where you belong. Great relationships never happen by accident. And that includes our relationship with God.

KEY THOUGHT

Everyone's relationship with God ends up somewhere, but few relationships with God end up somewhere on purpose. Your past often holds the key to unlock your future.

God wants you hot! But hot only happens on purpose.

36

WHAT'S YOUR TEMPERATURE?

Steve became a Christ-follower six months ago. With God's help, he overcame an addiction to methamphetamines and alcohol. As a new believer, Steve has led four family members to Christ, participates in two small groups, serves in our children's ministry weekly, participates in a men's prayer breakfast, and has been to three countries on missions trips. All this in six months. Steve told me he is only beginning.

> Before long, he convinced everyone at the party to raise their beers...and make a toast "to Pastor Craig."

This man is hot!

Then there's Mike. Mike is a good friend of mine. But he is not yet a follower of Christ. God would call him cold. He is not a bad guy. Quite the opposite. He is honest, loyal, dependable, and just plain likable. But he's never been born anew spiritually.

When Mike was twelve, he found his mom dead in the bathtub after one of her seizures. Mike finds it difficult to believe in a God who would allow that to happen. I can understand his struggles. He goes to church. He's open to God to a point. Just not to the point of relational commitment.

Mike also likes to party.

One night, Mike was throwing a wild party. Everyone there was wasted. Someone started making fun of preachers. My name came up. As several intoxicated people started to bash me, Mike jumped in and defended me. He told them I was the "real deal." Before long, he convinced everyone at the party to raise their beers...and make a toast "to Pastor Craig."

Did I mention that I like Mike?

Jesus said to one guy, "You are not far from the kingdom of God" (Mark 12:34). Mike is not far. But he's cold.

Still, it's better to be cold...than lukewarm.

Another friend (I'll call him Travis) was once passionate about his relationship with God. In his business, he had a bold yet gentle way of sharing his faith, leading many to Christ. He was known as a person of integrity and was even an elder in his church. Travis taught Sunday school, volunteered with youth, and was raising three great kids.

Then one day he started to drift.

His wife said she noticed a few small

> One day he started to drift. His wife said she noticed a few small signs but didn't think much of them.

signs but didn't think much of them. He first started watching movies he previously considered bad for his faith. Then he stopped reading his Bible and dropped his men's accountability meetings. To most people, everything seemed normal on the outside. But on the inside, something had changed.

One day, Travis had lunch with a woman in his office. He enjoyed her company and she enjoyed his. What seemed innocent at first quickly slid into a series of destructive decisions.

With a cooling passion for God, Travis betrayed his covenant vows with God and his wife by committing adultery.

I wish I could tell you he repented, his wife forgave him, and his kids are doing fine. The truth is not so pleasant. Travis left his wife for this woman. Their relationship didn't work out.

Travis's wife is trying to rebuild a life of shattered dreams. His children have not spoken to him for two years. He drinks himself into a stupor night after night. Alone. Hurting.

He occasionally attends church, but he has a faraway look in his eyes.

Travis's faith became lukewarm.

THE ANSWER IS ALREADY YES

Remember junior high? If a boy liked a girl, he was usually too terrified to ask her out. After all, she might say no. So he would ask another girl to ask her friend if, by chance, the girl he liked might, hypothetically speaking, say yes.

Up the chain the boy's question would travel. Then back down the chain all the way the girl's answer would come: *Yes!*

The boy would then faint.

You don't have to play that game with God.

God has already said *yes*.

"'You will seek me and find me when you seek me with all your heart. *I will be found by you*,' declares the LORD" (Jeremiah 29:13–14, emphasis mine, but God's as well, I believe).

> Even after you've sought God and known Him for a lifetime, He'll still say, "Yes, come even closer."

God wants you to seek Him. And when you do, He will reveal the depths of His character, His nature, His glory. In ways you can't imagine.

Even after you've sought God and known Him for a lifetime, He'll still say, "Yes, come even closer. There's much more of Me to find."

And even if you've run from Him for a lifetime, He'll still say yes.

His answer is always yes.

YOU CAN GET CLOSER TO GOD

There's a spiritual law that holds great promise for anyone ready to experience more intimacy with God. Think of it as the Principle of Compound Motion: When you move, God moves too.

You move closer to God, He will move closer to you. "Come near to God and he will come near to you," we read in James 4:8. Anyone who wants to can get closer to God.

Are you ready to make your move?

Two questions will help you move closer to God, rather than drift away.

The first one is, *What disciplines best help you experience God?*

I try to avoid a one-formula-fits-all mentality. I don't want you thinking that if you just check off the Bible study box or the prayer box, you've met with God. God is so much bigger than that. And He has given you so many more ways of enjoying His presence.

> Are you ready
> to make your move?

Yet there are certain basic ingredients that make for a strong relationship with God. Just about all cakes are made with flour and water. But the number of ways to build on the basics is endless.

And so it is with God and us. While all followers of Christ walk in the same direction to grow closer to God, their paths can be very different.

Some common spiritual disciplines include Bible study, prayer, fasting, worship, fellowship with other believers, accountability, service, and outreach. These are basic ingredients for a life lived close to God's heart. A hot life.

But each of these essential habits can be practiced in a variety of ways. Potentially an endless variety. Feel free to experience God in creative, uncommon ways. For you these might end up being the most important part of your relationship with God.

Any parent will relate in unique ways to each of his or her children.

My oldest daughter and I experience love by reading together. My second daughter and I like to use little hand gestures that are only known to the two of us. My third daughter and I like to talk. And talk. And talk. My oldest son and I wrestle and squish bugs. (When he's twenty-two, I suspect—I hope—we'll connect differently, but no less genuinely.) My second son and I relate by singing and snuggling. And with my youngest, I tell her a short story before bedtime and every night she tells me I'm her favorite daddy. (As far as I know I'm her only daddy, but I'm still thankful I'm her favorite.)

Give yourself permission to connect with your Father in uncommon ways—ways that are unique to you. For instance, maybe you would enjoy journaling your prayers. Or praying conversationally during a walk. You can add the YouVersion Bible app to your phone and read it whenever you have downtime. If you don't enjoy reading, you can get an audio version of the Bible and listen to it everywhere you go.

Be creative. Get out of the box. Ask yourself, *How can I best experience God?* And then practice what works for you. At different times in your life it may change.

The bottom line is to pursue God passionately.

And if you were once hot but you've drifted, Jesus says, "You have forsaken your first love.... Repent and do the things you did at first" (Revelation 2:4–5).

Ease back into the old, good habits. Have a reunion with your Father.

The second question to guide you toward God is, *What barriers are hindering you from experiencing God?*

David said in Psalm 24:4–5, "He who has clean hands and a pure heart, who does not lift up his soul to an idol or swear by what is false. He will receive blessing from the LORD."

In this passage, we see two major barriers. The first one is "dirty hands," or *sin*.

When I was a kid, my mom used to say, "Craig, after you use the restroom, always wash your hands." Sometimes I faked it. I don't know why. I'd turn on the water, but I wouldn't get my hands wet. Pretty dumb, huh?

Many of us are faking our spiritual hygiene. Your spouse may not know. Your friends may not know. But you and God know. Unconfessed sin is in your heart. Your hands are dirty.

In the New Testament, one Greek word for sin is *hamartia*. It means "to miss the mark." Sin doesn't have to be intentional. It's the default mode for humans most of the time. And it is what happens nearly always when you don't intentionally seek God, when you aren't living on purpose.

Paul wrote to the Corinthian church, "Come back to your senses as you ought, and stop sinning" (1 Corinthians 15:34). Confess your sin. Turn away from it and let the fire of God's Spirit cleanse you from anything that hinders your relationship with Him.

It's the only sensible thing to do.

Confession isn't easy, but it's absolutely critical. I confess any sins—even the grossest—to my wife and to my accountability partner. Their prayers are the reason I've made progress overcoming those sins. And the reason I enjoy God as much as I do today.

> An idol is anything that we put before God.

I dare you to be honest. I double dog dare you. What sin is hindering your relationship with God? Maybe for you it is pride or self-sufficiency. How about lust or gossip? Maybe it is a combination of materialism and greed. Perhaps for you it is some addiction. You claim you can stop whenever you want to. Why haven't you?

And in case you've felt trapped by a habitual, repetitive sin, here's some encouragement: "God is faithful; he will not let you be tempted beyond what you can bear. But when you are tempted, he will also provide a way out so that you can stand up under it" (1 Corinthians 10:13).

No sin is too big for God to conquer in you. God will show you a way out.

David mentioned a second barrier to experiencing God. It's *idolatry*. Think of idolatry not as a single act of sin but as a lifestyle built around sinful priorities.

One of the Ten Commandments says, "You shall have no other gods before me" (Exodus 20:3). An idol is anything that we put before God.

Some of us put our hobbies ahead of God. Some people devote more time to watching television every day than they spend with God in a month. And need I point out the tyranny of money?

Our careers can become idols.

We can even put our children ahead of God.

Other idols today? Our appearance, our bodies, our health, our possessions, our pride. Anything we value can become more valuable to us than God. Even good things. That's when it becomes an idol.

> Give yourself permission to connect with your Father in uncommon ways.

What are you most tempted to put ahead of God?

What are the disciplines that best help you experience God? (The ones that draw you closer.)

What are the barriers that hinder your relationship with God? (The ones that push you further away.)

In other words, what do you need to start or stop doing to burn with passion for God?

YOU'RE THE AUTHOR

Your Relationship with God

I do promise God that I will rise early every morning
to have a few minutes—not less than five—in private prayer.... I hereby vow to read no less than four
chapters in God's Word every day. I will cultivate a
spirit of self-denial, and I will yield myself a prisoner
of love to the Redeemer of the world.

—WILLIAM BOOTH, *founder of the Salvation Army*

As one of my personal goals, I have committed to read through the Bible
every year. I have promised God to lead my family spiritually. This includes praying with them, discipling them according to the core values God
has given us, and formal yet fun creative family devotions.

REFLECTION

What specific, attainable, written goals will you set for yourself in your pursuit of God?

1. **Draw Me Closer.** What disciplines best help you experience God?
   Remember to think outside of the box. (Hint: What has brought
   you close to God in the past? What is something new that might
   draw you to Him in a fresh way?)

   Short-Term Goals: Now write one or two specific, attainable
   goals to help you develop your relationship with God. (These
   goals should be related to your responses to question 1.)

2. **Push Me Further Away.** What are the barriers hindering you from experiencing God? Write down any sin that needs cleansing. List anything you are putting before God. Be honest.

   Short-Term Goals: Write one or two specific goals to remove barriers from your relationship with God. (For example, if you are looking at pornography on your computer, commit to get a filtered Internet. Or if you are too busy to spend daily time with God, commit to get up thirty minutes earlier and make it happen.)

3. **Very Next Step.** Now describe the specific action you will take to realize your goals. Provide names, time frames, specific steps, or phone calls—whatever it will take for you to follow through. Pray and thank God that He is inviting you into a closer relationship with Him. Ask Him for the courage and commitment to pursue genuine intimacy with Him with purpose and passion.

What do you want to do next? If you're ready to continue and create an action plan in another fundamental life area, read on.

But maybe you want to take the goals you've already established and live them out for a while before considering action plans for other areas. If that's the case, it's important for you to read the last part of the book. Please skip ahead to page 193, and finish reading the book from that point.

For more resources, visit www.chazown.com.

RELATIONSHIPS WITH PEOPLE

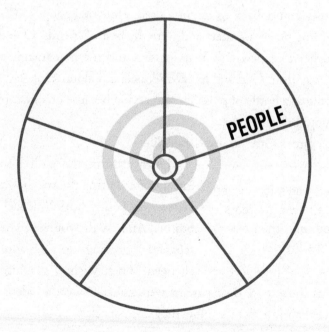

39

OBSERVATIONS ALONG THE PATH

I'm walking along a forest path. I think I might be dreaming, but I'm not sure. Ahead I notice two pieces of paper moving slightly in the breeze. I realize they're two halves of an old torn photograph. Sarah was in her twenties and smiling ear to ear. Her arm was draped around her slightly older best friend, Holly.

The story comes back to me in a flash. Holly led Sarah to Christ. They quickly became prayer partners and were the best of friends. One day Sarah's job moved her to a new city. Years passed, and the best friends lost touch. Sarah fell away from God and felt abandoned and alone. One day, she found herself staring at a bottle of pills. She was crying because no one cared. Maybe the pills could bring her rest.

The picture is torn. So was Sarah's life.

> One day Sarah's job moved her to a new city. Years passed, and the best friends lost touch.

Further down the path I see another torn photo. Putting the two halves together, I view two young boys. Michael is the big brother, Andrew the younger. They were inseparable growing up. As adults, things changed. When Michael was thirty-four and Andrew was thirty-two, their parents were killed in a car accident. The boys fought over their inheritance. Now they don't speak.

Two more torn lives.

Off to the side, I notice two more pieces of paper. No. Too much pain. I don't want to look. But I do.

It's Keith and Daniel, father and son. Daniel had his dad's green eyes. He idolized his daddy. His daddy idolized his job, leaving no time for his son. One day the emotionally starved young man left home. "For good," he said.

"Enough!" I protest. "No more!"

Then I see Larry and his wife, Peggy. In the picture they look perfect, smiling, standing together outside their suburban home. No one knew Larry had another life. His sin ripped apart his wife's heart. They stayed together for a while, but finally she couldn't take it anymore, and she left him.

Suddenly, I awake from the dream. Heart pounding. Soaked in sweat. Only to realize the stories are true.

40

VIEWING PEOPLE WITH PURPOSE

We all have relationships that could be better. Some of us have relationships that couldn't be much worse. Whatever the condition of your connections with people, God provides clear guidance for improving them. He has a dream, especially for your bonds with those closest to you.

God wants to reveal His will, His dream for our relationships, because…

KEY THOUGHT
Where there is no vision for our relationships with people, those relationships will wither and perish.

God is a God of relationships. And He hates it when relationships perish.

Relationships reflect the very heart of God. When He created the world, He said everything was good except for one thing: It was not good for man to be alone. And yet so many live without an intentional relational plan.

Some would argue, "I'm not alone. I'm with people all the time." The strange truth is that one can be in a crowded room of people and still be alone. Or be married for forty years and be little more than roommates. Or go to church every week and talk about loving the lost while not even knowing your next-door neighbor's name.

God wants us to experience His fullness through great relationships. He has people prepared to mentor you, sharpen you, love you, and lead you toward His Chazown for your life. He also prepared you to speak into the lives of others. To make them better and more effective. He has accountability friends prepared to be a blessing in your life. God has plans to bless your favorite relationships and glorify His name as you share His love.

But it will take an intentional, prayerful step on your part.

For years I didn't see the value of intentionally developing godly relationships. That was my wife's department, so I left the relational ball in her court. Content with following along, I struggled relationally, not seeing the value of investing in and receiving from them.

Then it dawned on me. God's greatest command is to love Him. His second greatest is to love His people. Everything is about relationships. And every aspect of your Chazown will be strengthened and blessed by the right relationships.

> He has people prepared to mentor you, sharpen you, love you, and lead you toward His Chazown for your life.

Together we'll seek God, and our relationships will end up where He wants them to be.

KEY THOUGHT
Every relationship ends up somewhere, but few relationships end up somewhere on purpose.

Let's talk about how to build relationships on purpose.

41

CHAZOWN AND GOOD COMPANY

I offer you four questions to help you grasp and live God's chazown for your relationships:

The first question is, *What relationship needs to be initiated?*

We all need people for support, encouragement, accountability. Who is missing for you? Who does God want in your life to help you achieve your life's purpose?

Ecclesiastes 4:9–10 says, "Two are better than one, because they have a good return for their work: If one falls down, his friend can help him up. But pity the man who falls and has no one to help him up!"

So much of life trains us to do things solo. Most students study alone. They take tests alone. Graduates search for jobs alone. Couples try to have good marriages without the help of others. They try to raise kids alone. The kids grow up and raise their kids in the same kind of isolation. And the cycle continues.

God wants us to do life *together*—in a faith community, in a web of committed relationships, in teams.

But teams don't happen on accident. That's why my wife and I have intentionally initiated relationships and built our lives around teams. In our finances we rely on several consultants for advice. We have recruited people we value and trust to invest in our children's lives.

And our marriage is a result of great mentors. Like Rich and Anna. They have one of the strongest marriages of any couple we know. So as a newly married couple, we asked them to mentor us, and they agreed. Not only did they model generous giving, fighting fairly, and communicating deeply, but more than anything, we learned to have fun as a married couple.

Not too long ago, we invested in a young couple, Rocky and Lydia. They were students, well on their way to a blessed marriage. Lydia says that Amy taught her how to submit healthily to Rocky's leadership while still contributing her insight to the marriage. Rocky says he learned to better lead and make financial plans. This couple knows the value of teams, asking others to speak into their lives. They know great relationships don't happen by accident.

When we depend on God's people, we're depending on Him, because people are one of His key tools for working in our lives.

But here's a key: You have to look for these relationships; *don't wait for them to come to you.* Jesus didn't wait for the twelve disciples to come to Him; He chose them.[12]

> Ask God. Pray for those missing relationships.

What relationship do you need to initiate? Maybe you need a close Christian friend for support, to battle alongside you. Maybe you need to get into a small group. Maybe you need an accountability partner. Maybe you need a date. (Just joking. Well, maybe not.)

Quit waiting for someone to come to you, to take you under their wing or ask to be your friend. Go ask them.

And ask God. Pray for those missing relationships. "You do not have, because you do not ask God" (James 4:2).

Intentionally chosen relationships are critical for your fulfillment of God's Chazown for you.

42

AS GOOD AS IT GETS?

The second question for guiding your relationships with people is, *What relationship needs to be nurtured?*

How does a friendship go from bosom buddies and finishing each other's sentences to "we're not speaking"?

How does a marriage go from "all the songs on the radio are about us" to a court hearing?

How does a marriage go from "all the songs on the radio are about us" to a court hearing?

The reason our important relationships go south is because we fail to purposefully nurture them.

My wife, Amy, and I strongly agree: Our marriage is as good as we want it to be. Not as good as *I* want it to be. Not as good as *she* wants it to be. But as good as *we*—in cooperative effort—want it to be. If we neglect our relationship, it's not pretty. If we invest in it, it's six kids good. When we guard it and make each other's needs a priority, you would not believe the spiritual intimacy, the depth of friendship, the level of intense vulnerability. It is the richest human relationship I've ever known.

But when we let it slide—get too busy or distracted—you would not believe how quickly we start to struggle.

How do you nurture a relationship? You "serve one another in love," because "the entire law is summed up in a single command: 'Love your neighbor as yourself.'" But "if you keep on biting and devouring each other, watch out or you will be destroyed by each other" (Galatians 5:13–15).

Every relationship ends up somewhere, but few relationships end up somewhere on purpose.

If you let your relationship take its natural course, you'll eat away at each other until the relationship is destroyed. You must choose to serve one another in love.

Let's say your marriage needs nurturing. What do you do? Do something different than what you've been doing. Maybe you will commit to biblical counseling. Maybe you'll let a wiser, older couple speak into your marriage. Or start praying together or reading the Bible together. Or join a supportive small group together. Or read a book on communication together. Or turn up the heat on your physical intimacy.

> If you let your relationship take its natural course, you'll eat away at each other until the relationship is destroyed. You must choose to serve one another in love.

Seek God and let Him guide you in nurturing your marriage toward your chazown for that relationship. Otherwise, your marriage may end up somewhere you won't like.

Say you have a strained relationship with your son or daughter. What do you do? Do something different. Find an activity you enjoy together. Ask and answer questions. Write notes to each other. Take your child on a trip, just the two of you. Start praying together.

Say you have allowed a wall of resentment to separate you from a co-worker or a neighbor. What do you do? Begin by owning your part of the problem—the attitudes, the gossip, the limited perspective. Then own most of the other person's part of the problem too. Initiate sincere apologies. Affirm wherever possible. Ask God to break down the barriers. Keep taking steps in the right direction. Then let God be sovereign over the outcome.

Maybe you're not on speaking terms with an extended family member. Have a friend hold you accountable to call the relative once a month, send an e-mail, or have lunch with him or her.

Healing can take time. Be patient. Keep trying. And don't give up.

Whatever it is, it must be your conscious, deliberate decision—an *intentional* relationship.

I love what one of our church's small groups does. The wives get together one Saturday a month to nurture and disciple their daughters. They collectively expose the girls to things they enjoy, such as learning to cook, studying about courtship, or taking nature hikes.

At the same time, the husbands gather to invest in their sons by doing service projects together. They select a person who needs help, go to his or her home, and ask, "What do you need done?"

> It must be your conscious, deliberate decision—an intentional relationship.

These families do life together through relationships that have been purposefully initiated and nurtured.

Serve one another in love.

Seek God, and ask Him—and yourself—what relationship in your life needs to be nurtured.

43

BIBLICAL BRIDGE REPAIR

Discovering God's chazown for your relationships involves a third question. And it's a tough one: *What relationship needs to be restored?*

Be honest with God about this.

Think about the relationships in your life that are broken, damaged, wounded. In some cases, you've been offended. In some, you're the offender.

Maybe you haven't honored one or both of your parents. Maybe your parents have done something to hurt you.

Perhaps *you're* the parent, but you've written off one of your children because of decisions that hurt or embarrassed you.

Has someone at work gotten under your skin, and you're holding a grudge?

Is one of your friendships strained?

Ask God what relationship needs to be restored.

> Think about the relationships in your life that are broken, damaged, wounded.

Colossians 3:13 says, "Bear with each other and forgive whatever grievances you may have against one another. Forgive as the Lord forgave you."[13] Who are we to hold anything against another person when God has forgiven us infinitely?

Jesus also taught that we should initiate restoration when *we* have wronged someone. "If you are offering your gift at the altar [that means worshiping God] and there remember that your brother has something against you, leave your gift there in front of the altar. First go and be reconciled to your brother; then come and offer your gift" (Matthew 5:23–24).

You may have little hope for healing your broken relationship. But remember, all things are possible with God (see Matthew 19:26). God is the

God of restoration. The Old Testament Hebrew word *shuwb* is translated "restored." It means "better than new." That's our goal for damaged relationships. Have faith in God. He can make your relationship even better than new.

You may feel nervous or even afraid to attempt restoration. I can relate. One of my most important relationships crumbled to the point that I believed it would never be repaired.

This friend was one of the most important people in my life. (I'll call him Rick.) After years of strong friendship, Rick thought I betrayed him. I thought I was doing the right thing. In his mind, I was the worst person who ever lived. A Judas. To me, he was narrow-minded, judgmental, and overlooking what's most important. No matter who was right, it got embarrassingly ugly. My once-close friend *hated* me. And he let everyone know it.

Several times I attempted restoration with Rick. Each time, I was met with a door slammed in my face. Finally, I gave up, convinced we would never again be close.

And the relationship sat broken for several long and pain-filled years.

One day during my prayer time, God gave me a small nudge. *Try again.*

No way, I thought. *Forget it. I won't subject myself to his abuse.*

Try again. I couldn't shake the thought.

Fearing another harsh and humiliating encounter, I finally made the phone call. To my shock and amazement, Rick agreed to meet. When we did, it was only minutes before we were mutually apologizing, hugging, and celebrating a restored relationship.

Now I barely remember the ugly details. It's almost as if they never occurred. God made our friendship better than new.

It is possible that, despite your best effort, the other person will refuse to reconcile. But *you* are the only person who answers to God for *you.* Paul wrote, "Do not repay anyone evil for evil. Be careful to do what is right in the eyes of everybody. *If it is possible, as far as it depends on you,* live at peace with everyone" (Romans 12:17–18).

Have you done everything within your power to seek restoration? Look past the pain to the potential pleasure of relationships that are everything God wants them to be. Your relational chazown.

Try again.

44

GOOD FRIEND, BAD FRIEND

Jessica and Jenny were inseparable twins, dressing alike and sharing their parents' faith in Christ. Both were morally strong. Their futures were bright with possibilities.

Here is the story of the summer things changed.

Jessica followed family tradition. As in years past, she attended a Christian camp. This year she made friends with some missions-minded girls. They didn't talk a lot about boys or music or movies. They talked about impacting the world. Feeding the poor. Reaching the lost.

In her church, Jessica was known as a strong Christian. But her new friends seemed to have a turbocharged faith. When these young girls prayed, they *really* prayed. During free time, they often read their Bibles. They talked of God as if He was a close friend, loving and directing them moment by moment. Jessica was caught by their passion.

Late in the summer, Jessica agreed to travel with her new friends to Tegucigalpa, Honduras, to build homes for the poor and tell people about Jesus.

That experience changed Jessica's life forever. After two years of college, she took a year off to minister in Honduras. There she met Rob. They later got married, and now they serve in China as full-time missionaries. Jessica glows with the love of Christ.

That same summer was also a fateful one for Jenny.

Instead of attending Christian camp, Jenny talked her mom, Monica, into letting her stay with a family at their beach house along with several other girls from school. Monica hesitated, because she didn't know the family well. But she gave in. For the rest of her life, Monica would regret this decision.

At first, Jenny was taken aback by this family's behavior. The parents gave the teenage girls beer. Lots of beer.

For a week, Jenny watched, not participating with the wild crowd. They seemed to be having so much fun. After several nights of pressure from her friends, Jenny drank her first beer. The next night, she got drunk. The night after that, she smoked pot.

That was only the beginning. Jenny met an older guy by the water. On the last night of the trip, drunk and high, Jenny gave away her virginity.

> Having discovered new friends who were more "fun" than the church crowd, Jenny was different when she returned home.

Having discovered new friends who were more "fun" than the church crowd, Jenny was different when she returned home. More sophisticated. More grown-up. And more prone to trouble.

Today, Jenny is an alcoholic on her third marriage, raising children from her first two husbands and a third man she met in a bar. Tonight she will sleep in a women's shelter.

And her mom will cry herself to sleep.

Two sisters. Two sets of friends. Two drastically divergent destinations.

Leading us to the fourth question...

45

DROPPING DEAD WEIGHT

I considered not including this question in this book because of the ways it can be misconstrued. But after praying, I decided it was important enough to risk.

Question number four: *What relationship needs to be severed?*

Let me make very clear what I am *not* saying by this question. I'm not talking about divorce on unbiblical grounds, no matter how unhappy you are in your marriage. And I'm not talking about cutting off a taxing, often-unrewarding relationship you *know* before God you're responsible to sustain.

> I am talking about wrong, destructive, and unhealthy relationships that need to be severed. Or at least redefined.

What I am talking about are wrong, destructive, and unhealthy relationships that need to be severed. Or at least redefined.

Paul warned us in 1 Corinthians 15:33, "Do not be misled: 'Bad company corrupts good character.'"

My mom always said, "Craig, you are who you run with." I hated it when she said that. Probably because she was right.

If you are a single adult trying to decide whether a potential boyfriend or girlfriend has good character, check out his or her friends. If he or she is keeping good company—friends who are a positive influence—then you can expect a greater degree of authenticity. But if the friends are heading the wrong way, they're likely to drag anyone attached to them along for the ride.

In the same letter to the Corinthians, Paul wrote, "You must not associate with anyone who calls himself a brother but is sexually immoral or greedy, an idolater or a slanderer, a drunkard or a swindler. With such a man do not even eat" (1 Corinthians 5:11). If you're in a relationship that is hurting your relationship with God, either redefine it or lovingly, tactfully break it off until the person has *genuinely* changed.

You have a business partner who lacks integrity. End or redefine the arrangement.

You have a friend who spiritually drags you down. Redefine the friendship or sever it.

Guys, you hang around buddies who trash-talk their wives, and it's hurting your marriage. Either the boys change their habits, or you're out.

> Why enjoy the thrill when you know where it's leading?

Ladies, you're running with a bunch of man haters, gossipers, backbiters. Find another crowd. Don't let anyone damage your attitude toward your husband, brother, or father.

Watch out for people who are a source of temptation to you. Why enjoy the thrill when you know where it's leading? And if you're dating someone who is clearly not God's will for you, why waste your time? You could use it to meet the person who is God's perfect vision for your future! Why are you taking yourself off the market?

Seek God. Ask for His direction. And determine to do what He says, even if it's painful.

46

THE JOURNEY BACK

Another evening. Another dream. Back in the same forest with the same photographs. But something is different.

There are Sarah and Holly, the friends who lost touch. Staring down a bottle of pills, Sarah contemplated ending her life. At the same moment with over a thousand miles between them, Holly felt unusually moved to call her old and distant friend. Sarah's phone scared her back to reality with three loud rings. She hopelessly picked up the phone only to hear her old friend say, "God had you on my heart, so I thought I'd call."

The torn picture pieces had now become one. And so had these two friends.

Then I saw Peggy and Larry, the man with the secret life. The next chapter of their story flashes into my mind. When Peggy left Larry, Larry hit bottom. He called out to God. And God changed his heart. After breaking off the wrong relationships, he confessed all of his sins to God and his wife. Miraculously, Peggy took him back. Today their marriage is what God wants it to be.

Then I realize what's different. The two halves of the picture are glued back together. I can hardly tell it was once torn.

> The torn picture pieces had now become one. And so had these two friends.

Someone has also repaired the picture of the two brothers. Three years after the fight, Andrew realized nothing was worth losing the love he once shared with Michael. He took a chance and made a call. He apologized to his brother, and the two are once again inseparable.

Then I see the father and son. When Daniel was fifteen, Keith lost the job he idolized. Suddenly Daddy had to ask himself what was most important in life. Today this father and son are back in the relationship God intended them to have.

Every relationship ends up somewhere. But few relationships end up somewhere on purpose.

YOU'RE THE AUTHOR

Your Relationships with People

Are you ready to write some more? Let's do it.

REFLECTION

Ask God to help you think through and answer the following four questions.

1. What relationship needs to be *initiated*? (Do you need a close friend, an accountability partner, a spiritual or business mentor? What key relationship is missing from your life?)

2. What relationship needs to be *nurtured*? (Does your marriage need improvement? Are you distant from a parent or a child? Have you drifted from a close friend?)

3. What relationship needs to be *restored*? (Who do you need to forgive? From whom do you need to seek forgiveness? What relationship has been damaged and needs restoration?)

4. What relationship needs to be *severed*? (Are you close to someone who is hurting your relationship with God? Or hurting your marriage? Are you dating someone who's not right for you? Do you have a friend who's dragging you down morally?)

SHORT-TERM GOALS

Now define one or two relational goals. Be specific.

VERY NEXT STEP

Now describe the specific action you will take to realize your goals. Provide names, time frames, specific actions—whatever it will take for you to follow through.

Pray and thank God that He is directing your relationships. Ask Him for the courage and commitment to handle these relationships with purpose.

What do you want to do next? If you're ready to continue and create an action plan in another life area, then read on.

But maybe you want to take the goals you've already established and live them out for a while before considering action plans in other areas. If that's the case, it's important for you to read the last part of the book. Please skip ahead to page 193 and finish reading the book from that point.

For more resources, visit www.chazown.com.

FINANCES

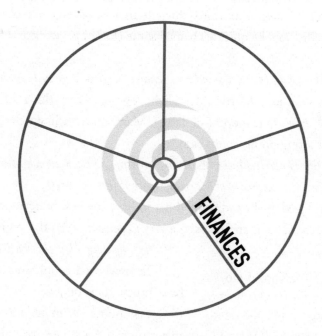

47

DISASTER DOWN UNDER

Once upon a time there was a college grad named Martin.

If you and I were observers standing near Martin throughout his life, we would see him holding a figurative shovel, standing on the lawn of life.

Martin left college with thirty-three thousand dollars in school debt. After landing his first job, he quickly charged some clothes for work and financed a new car.

Dig. The shovel breaks the sod and removes its first large heap of dirt.

At his new job, Martin met Shelli. She was everything he had ever dreamed of. After nine months of dating, Martin and Shelli were engaged. He bought her a ring on his credit card.

Dig. Dig. The shovel moves more dirt, creating a hole in which Martin is knee deep. But he seems unaware of his steady descent into the earth.

Martin loved Shelli and wanted her to have the best honeymoon. He increased his credit limit and charged a very expensive seven-day cruise.

Dig. Dig. Dig. Now the hole is waist deep.

The newlywed couple was shocked at how much they qualified to borrow for

> Dig. Dig. The shovel moves more dirt, creating a hole in which Martin is knee deep. But he seems unaware of his steady descent.

their first home. With no money down, they purchased a house that was as large and nice as Martin's parents' home. One month after they moved in, Shelli's car broke down. The couple purchased a new one on a convenient seventy-two-month loan.

Dig. Dig. Dig. Dig. We can barely see the top of Martin's head. Oblivion continues to reign.

Shelli bought new drapes for the house. Martin bought a desk for his office. Then the roof needed replacing. The water heater broke. And when they found out the house had furnace problems, the couple decided to have the repairman install air-conditioning as well.

Deeper and deeper becomes the hole. In fact, we now realize that Martin cannot possibly get out by himself.

Before either of them had reached thirty, Martin and Shelli filed for bankruptcy.

The statistics are sobering. Did you know that 75 percent of Christians live paycheck to paycheck every month, always fearfully wondering if they're going to have enough?

And the average twenty-eight-year-old has sixty-six thousand dollars in consumer debt! (Let that sink in.)

To make matters even scarier, only 38 percent of Americans pay off their credit card bills each month. That means 62 percent...don't.

> Seventy-five percent of Christians live paycheck to paycheck every month, always fearfully wondering if they're going to have enough.

How do Americans compare with the rest of the world? Recently, the Japanese saved 18 percent of their income. Americans? We went in the hole 2.2 percent.

Someone said, "If you fail to plan, you plan to fail."

Maybe that's why so many people end up...in the hole.

KEY THOUGHT
When it comes to finances,
everyone ends up somewhere.
But few people end up somewhere on purpose.

48

THE SPIRITUAL SIDE OF MONEY

Finances may seem like a very unspiritual topic. Yet two-thirds of Jesus' parables spoke directly about money or possessions. In the Gospels, one of every ten verses addresses financial issues. In all of Scripture, over 2,300 verses talk about money.

Why did Jesus focus so much on money? Perhaps He knew that material and financial distractions could become God's leading competitor for our hearts, attention, and affection.

God's message is clear. Without clear thinking and wise planning, every one of us is susceptible to bondage to money—a millionaire as much as a homeless person.

God wants to own our hearts. But for many, money (or the creditors) becomes what owns us instead of God. And our Father wants us to be free and to have no other "gods" before Him. How can you and I pursue our God-given Chazown when someone or something else lords over us? If we're in debt, we're slaves, and not slaves to Christ.

Money matters to God because it reveals our values and the direction of our affection.

Money matters to you. I can't think of many issues that, when poorly managed, cause more pain and turmoil. Money can wreck a marriage, ruin someone's health through stress and panic, even turn a person's heart against God. That's why I believe the wise use of your finances is one of the most important spiritual issues in your life!

Have you ever noticed how society sets up young people to fail at money management? We teach students to make good grades so they can go to college…so they can get a good job…so they can make lots of money. But when they get to college, what greets them? A gauntlet of credit card stands luring them to sign up for their own personal plastic. Colleges also freely connect students with government loans that are often more than the student needs for tuition and costs.

Add a new car, too many late-night pizzas, the fall formal, and the spring break trip, and you have a formula for financial catastrophe.

These young graduates exit college upside down on their cars and dragging along twenty to forty thousand dollars of college debt. And they have no clue how they got there!

Welcome to the real world.

Perhaps that's why 19 percent of the bankruptcies filed just a few years ago were filed by college students.

The topic of financial responsibility requires far more detailed instruction than I can provide in a few chapters. I also realize

> Why did Jesus focus so much on money?

that many good people are in dire financial need not of their own making, and with no good options on the horizon. For that reason, I'll later direct you to other excellent resources on the topic. My hope here is to inspire you to prayerfully seek God's chazown for your financial life. If I light a fire under you and you go looking for sound financial direction, then this part of my book will have served its purpose.

49

CHAZOWN AND CASH

R eady to see your finances in a new way? Then spend some time prayerfully thinking through some important questions:

Where do you think God wants you to be financially one year from now?
Would He have you eliminate some debt? Pay off your credit cards? Establish
a savings account? Create and live by a bud-
get? Change some spending habits?

> Where do you think God
> wants you to be financially
> one year from now?

How about in five years? Does He want
you to have money put aside for a large ex-
pense you would otherwise buy with credit?
Perhaps you could be free of all debt. Might you give 15 percent of your income
instead of 10?

And twenty years down the road? Maybe then God wants you so financially free that you'll live off a small fraction of your wealth and give substan-
tially to His work—in your community or on the other side of the world or
both.

I've been asking a lot of money questions that add up to one critical, big-
picture question: *What is your financial vision?*

K EY THOUGHT
Where there is no financial vision,
most people end up in the hole.

Someone once said, "The average American drives his bank-financed car
over a bond-financed highway on credit card gas to open a charge account at
a department store so he can fill his financed home with installment-plan
furniture."[14]

Is that God's vision for you?

Or might it be something different? Something strange?

When it comes to finances, "normal" is not good. "Normal" is worried sick about money. "Normal" is fighting over financial challenges. "Normal" is car payments, credit card payments, and mortgages.

Dave Ramsey, a great Christian teacher on finances and close friend, often says, "I'll teach you to live like no one else, so that one day you can live like no one else." That's why I don't want normal. I want something weird. Something that flouts the world's conventional thinking.

> When it comes to finances, "normal" is not good.

Debt free. No payments. No interest. No worries. No burdens. No fear.

Is your vision to become financially free? Or do you want to join the majority — in the hole?

YOU CAN TURN AROUND

Consider two financial visions for your future:

Vision #1: For the rest of your life, you struggle financially. You live in fear, one emergency away from financial destruction. You never know whether your paycheck will cover the bills. Some months it doesn't. You and your spouse constantly fight over money—that is, as long as your marriage lasts. You suffer from stress. You envy those who are financially comfortable, but their lifestyle is something you will never know. You believe you are unable to tithe to God. You seem to be under an inescapable curse. You will always work, never able to retire. "You have planted much, but have harvested little. You eat, but never have enough. You drink, but never have your fill. You put on clothes, but are not warm. You earn wages, only to put them in a purse with holes in it" (Haggai 1:6).

If my insinuation that this could be your future offends you, you might be shouting, "That's not my vision!" But odds are that is exactly the direction you're traveling.

Vision #2: You're completely debt free within ten years or less. No car payments. No credit card payments. Not even a house payment. You are not bound to a particular job (because income doesn't direct you). You have more than enough for your needs; you even enjoy certain luxuries as blessings from God. You pay cash for everything. You've been faithful with little, so God has entrusted you with much. You are therefore free to give as God leads you, even funding entire ministries. When you see someone in need, you immediately help. Your answer to God is simply yes. For the rest of your life.

Which of these visions would you like to choose for your financial future?

Everyone ends up somewhere. But few people end up somewhere on purpose.

Now, suppose I want to drive to Dallas, Texas (south from my home). But you find me on the freeway going north.

What advice would you give me?

Turn around! You're going the wrong direction!

Right?

I'm now lovingly telling you: If you don't have a financial chazown, then Vision #1 is your likely destination. Do something different. Turn around in the power and wisdom of God's Holy Spirit. If you do, you'll look back on this as the moment you made your financial U-turn. God will get the glory. And you and many others will be eternally glad.

> Listen, you can change. I've seen hundreds of men and women in every kind of financial trouble decide to turn around and start walking in a better direction.

Skeptical? Hopeless? Hearing that voice inside you saying you've tried to straighten out your finances hundreds of times and—at least for you—things are never going to change?

Listen, that's a lie. You can change. I've seen hundreds of men and women in every kind of financial trouble decide to turn around and start walking in a better direction. And they have.

And you can too.

We have a God who can do more than we can imagine (see Ephesians 3:20). Ask Him to change your expectations about what He can do.

It's not too late.

Turn around.

51

VALUES, VISION, VICTORY

How do you discover God's specific chazown for your financial future? Start by taking a prayerful look at your core values.

Remember core values? What is it that stirs righteous anger within you? What do you absolutely love? What do you stand for?

In the world of wealth, if you don't stand for something, you'll lay down your money for anything.

By now, you should have some idea of the core values God put within you. Now, define your financial vision according to those values.

And not, by the way, according to the values the world wants to impose on you. I'm sure you've noticed by now—everyone else has their own chazown for your money!

> I'm sure you've noticed by now—everyone else has their own chazown for your money!

The television store's chazown: "Your viewing experience isn't complete until you have an enormous flat screen."

The jeweler's chazown: "You don't really love her unless you buy the largest diamond your credit allows."

The restaurant's chazown: "You deserve a break today…"

The athletic club's chazown: "You haven't had a real workout until you're paying at least eighty dollars a month for it."

The travel agent's chazown: "Life isn't complete until you've cruised the Caribbean. Oh, you have?… As I always say, life isn't complete until you've traveled Europe."

The car dealer's chazown: "You're living in the twenty-first century and you only have two cars?"

The realtor's chazown: "You won't be happy until you own a new home with a bigger kitchen."

Define your financial vision according to the core values *God* has given you, not the values others want to impose upon you.

How does this play out? Let's say that physical health is one of your core values. Well, to afford a gym membership, your vision might include driving an old car.

Or maybe generosity is one of your highest priorities. To give as much as possible, your vision could be to save thousands of dollars by packing your lunch instead of eating out.

If you value Christian education for your children, your vision might involve working a second part-time job to afford private school.

For you, ensuring that your children have their mom at home may be very important, so you choose to live in a smaller house so she doesn't have to work to meet payments.

Why on earth would you choose old, small, and brown-bag, when the world says you need new, big, and the full-meal deal? Because your choices are consistent with *your* values. Others may say you're crazy to do without cable, Internet, a cell phone, or that four-dollar latte. But how highly will you value their opinion when you're completely debt free?

When Amy and I married, we prayerfully shaped our financial vision based on our core values. When kids came along, we valued Amy staying home. That may not be your core value, but it was ours. We also felt very strongly about becoming free from all debt, including mortgage. So we set a goal to do so in five years.

We bought a very inexpensive home, drove laughable cars, and for five years didn't buy a single item of clothing that didn't come from a garage sale. We didn't eat out without a buy-one-get-one-free coupon…and then only for someone's birthday. We didn't even exchange presents.

And people thought we were weird.

We *were* weird. But we were weird according to our values. And I felt especially weird—in the best sense of the word—when, on my twenty-eighth birthday, I held in my hand a mortgage promissory note stamped "PAID IN FULL."

Our financial chazown continues. Each year we increase our giving by 1 percent. And one day I expect to be a pastor without taking a salary.

Please understand—I'm not giving you these details of our personal financial picture to boast. We've made our share of embarrassing financial mistakes! Like buying a car sight unseen on eBay. (Ouch.) I'm telling you what I would say if we were out for coffee and working hard together to find a different financial future for you. I'm taking the risk of self-disclosure in case what I say can serve as a reference point, and hopefully an encouragement.

> Define your financial vision according to the core values God has given you, not the values others want to impose upon you.

My story with Amy is a reflection of what God has placed in our hearts—our core values and His dream for us. What has God placed in your heart?

Where there is no vision to be financially free, dreams perish.

52

CHAZOWN WITH LEGS

So the first critical, big-picture financial question was, *What is your financial vision?* That is, Where are you going? Here's the second big-picture question: *What is your financial plan?* In other words, How will you get there?

In your finances, if you fail to plan—to seek God for your financial goals—you are by default planning to fail.

If you have any expectations or hopes about your financial future, you'll only fulfill them by establishing an intentional plan of action.

And in setting up your plan, I strongly encourage you to get help. Even the most insightful people benefit from the advice of others. Proverbs 15:22 says, "Plans fail for lack of counsel, but with many advisers they succeed." In my financial life, I've invited input from a wide variety of people—some of them in person, and some of them indirectly, through books they've written or through other types of resources.

> In setting up your plan, I strongly encourage you to get help.

And speaking of resources, I promised I'd point you to some good ones. There are many excellent books, Web sites, and other sources of guidance available, but here are a few of my favorites:

- *The Millionaire Next Door* by Thomas J. Stanley and William D. Danko
- *Financial Peace* and *The Total Money Makeover,* both by Dave Ramsey
- *Master Your Money* and *Taming the Money Monster,* both by Ron Blue

- *The Treasure Principle* by Randy Alcorn
- www.daveramsey.com
- www.crown.org

Whatever you do in establishing your financial plan, be sure to ask wise people for advice.

And implement it.

53

GETTING TO THERE FROM HERE

Let me suggest three areas of your finances where you should seek God's vision and establish an action plan:

The first is *giving*. Jesus said, "It is more blessed to give than to receive" (quoted by Paul in Acts 20:35). If you think of giving as a sidelight in life, think again. God has entrusted you with tremendous wealth—especially if you live in the United States—and how you use it is very important to Him. There's a reason God said to give the *firstfruits* of our income to Him.[15] So first things first. Put giving at the top of your financial plan.

While the tithe—giving 10 percent of your income—is the yardstick for beginning givers, ask God whether more aggressive giving might be part of His chazown for you.

In case it's helpful, more self-disclosure: For my family's giving plan, we tithe first. Then, as additional offerings, we give toward the costs of starting new church campuses, to people who are in need, to missionaries, and to feed and care for several children around the world.

Part of our future vision is to help finance families who want to adopt but can't afford the costs.

Our offerings reflect our values.

Start with your core values and set up an action plan for your giving.

A quick word of caution: Whatever you do, please don't treat God like a cosmic slot machine. *If I give enough, I'll hit the financial jackpot.* Give out of love and obedience to the One who first gave to you. But don't use your giving as ploy to leverage God to fix your finances while you refuse to take responsibility for your own choices.

The second area for vision and planning is *debt elimination*. Far too many people know the frightening truth of Proverbs 22:7: "The rich rule over the poor, and the borrower is servant to the lender." The Hebrew word for *servant* means "slave." It implies that the indebted person is in bondage—shackled and unable to live freely.

If you've ever heard someone say, "We'd love to have more kids, but we have too much debt," that, sadly, is bondage. Or, "I'd love for my wife to stay home, but our payments are so high we can't afford it." Bondage. Or, "We'd love to provide our kids this once-in-a-lifetime experience, but then we couldn't pay our credit card bill." Again, bondage.

> The borrower is enslaved to the lender.

The borrower is enslaved to the lender.

So how do you eliminate debt? There are two basic ways. Spend less and earn more. Plan for these.

Maybe your plan involves a second job, at least for a while. Or maybe a higher-paying job.

Carefully examine where your money is going and look for ways to decrease any unnecessary leakage.

I also urge you to read *Financial Peace* by Dave Ramsey and learn about the "debt snowball." In less time than you think, you can find financial freedom.

What could you do for God's kingdom if you aggressively pursued some creative, practical plans...and became debt free?

A third area for financial vision and planning is the *future*. Here's my paraphrase of Proverbs 21:20: "The wise have wealth and luxury, but fools live paycheck to paycheck." Wisdom means holding back some of your money, not letting it all escape as soon as it comes.

Here are five future needs worth planning for:

1. Plan for *emergencies*. Seventy-eight percent of Americans put emergency expenses on their credit cards. Instead, you should set aside at least one thousand dollars in the "oh no" fund.

2. Plan for *future purchases*. If you know your car will soon need replacement, or Christmas is only four months away, put aside money now and plan to pay cash.

3. Plan for *college*. Did I mention I have six kids? Imagine how foolish I would be if I didn't plan to provide at least some help for their upcoming education costs.

4. Plan for *death*. I'm talking about life insurance, wills, and trusts. Seventy percent of Americans die without planning provision for their loved ones. Don't do that to your family.

5. Plan for *retirement*. Now personally, I think doing nothing in your later years is not biblical. But no matter how you choose to spend those years, you must plan now for your living expenses then.

Seek God. Then, as you draw up your plan, study your Three Circles—your core values, your spiritual gifts, your past experiences. Ask advice, if necessary. Then act.

Remember the story Jesus told about the servants who invested their talents and reaped a return? That's the thing about money: Act wisely and it grows. Do nothing, and you're already sliding toward want.

54

IT'S GOTTA HURT

I pray passionately you'll discover God's vision for your finances, and that it will ignite within you an unstoppable passion.

But harbor no illusions about the price you'll pay.

A fan once said to a champion golfer, "I'd love to play golf like you do."

The champion looked at the man and said, "No, you wouldn't."

Startled, the man said, "Oh yeah? I'd give anything to do what you do."

Again the pro golfer answered, "No, you wouldn't."

The fan persisted until the man explained. "So many people say that to me. But no one is willing to do what I did in order to do what I do. I used to get up at five a.m. every day and hit golf balls until my hands bled. I would hit and hit and hit and hit and continue practicing hours after everyone else was gone. No one is willing to do what I did, but everyone wants to do what I do."

> If you're not willing to do what they did, you won't be able to do what they're doing now.

We all want the end result of financial health, but the way to get there takes planning and discipline. When you receive God's vision for your financial future and you see others living it in the present, remember...if you're not willing to do what they *did*, you won't be able to do what they're *doing* now.

So establish a written plan and consistently work toward your financial chazown. And one day you'll look back at this moment and worship because you will be free from debt, and you'll spend the rest of your life blessing others with the resources God trusts to your care.

YOU'RE THE AUTHOR

Your Finances

In developing your financial plan, pick one or two of the following goals:
- Write a five-year financial vision. Don't worry about trying to sound like a financial planner. But try to describe your personal goals for key areas like building an emergency fund, paying off credit cards, eliminating debt, beginning a college savings plan, obtaining adequate life insurance, creating a will, etc.
- Write and follow a budget.
- Commit to seek financial advice. Be specific about what you need. You may need a mentor or to enroll in a financial class in your church. You may need tax or investment advice.
- Commit to tithe 10 percent of your income to your church.
- Prayerfully decide where to give above your tithe. Let the Holy Spirit and the values God placed within your heart guide you. Give with joy!
- Eliminate debt. Do some prayerful research. You may need to sell a car and buy a less expensive model. You may need to take a second job or stop eating out. You may need to have a garage sale or start selling everything but your pets on eBay. (Well, maybe you can sell your cats.) Get creative.
- Plan for the future. Be specific. For example, if you're responsible for a spouse or a family, you probably need term life insurance. Or the amount you have now may no longer be adequate. You may need to set up a will or save for college or plan for a vacation. Seek God and make wise plans for your future.
- Something else:

SHORT-TERM GOALS

Which one or two financials goals will you pursue? Write them down.

VERY NEXT STEP

Now describe the specific action you will take to realize your chosen goals. Provide names, time frames, specific actions—whatever it will take for you to follow through.

What do you want to do next? If you're ready to continue and create an action plan in another life area, then read on.

But maybe you want to take the goals you've already established and live them out for a while before considering action plans in other areas. If that's the case, it's important for you to read the last part of the book. Please skip ahead to page 193, and finish reading the book from that point.

For more resources, visit www.chazown.com.

HEALTH AND FITNESS

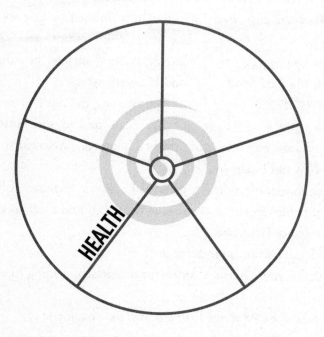

55

FAST FOOD FOR THOUGHT

The following is based on millions of true stories in all fifty states and the District of Columbia:

One day, Average American approached the drive-through of Fast Food Heaven. *What will it be today?* he thought to himself. *Maybe the supersized extra value deluxe combo meal special. Yeah, that's it.* Waiting in line, he sang the Fast Food Heaven jingle.

> Waiting in line, he sang the Fast Food Heaven jingle.

Approaching the outdoor menu, Average American pushed the button to roll down his window. The voice from the box boomed, "Welcome to Fast Food Heaven—how can I help you?"

Average American's stomach growled loudly in response. Salivating, he said, "I'd like the supersized extra value deluxe combo meal special, with a ninety-nine-ounce Dr Pepper."

"Would you like an apple pie with that?"

"No, thank you," Average American responded, priding himself on his restraint.

"Your total is $4.98 at the first window, sir. Thank you."

Fact: eight out of ten Americans over the age of twenty-five are overweight.

Average American grabbed the bag of food from the girl at the window, opened it, and stuffed a handful of French fries in his mouth. "Mank mou," he said gratefully around a mass of greasy chewed potato.

Fact: 60 percent of all Americans are either overweight or obese.

Using skills learned from his parents, Average American avoided wrecking his car as he simultaneously drove, talked on his cell phone with his investment advisor (about the exciting upward trend in fast food stocks), and ate the entire supersized extra value deluxe combo meal special.

Three miles down the road, he passed the Feel Healthy Gym.

"Maybe I should start working out," said Average American. He meditated on this inspiring idea for the whole twelve seconds that it took for the gym to pass out of view. Then a more inspiring idea crowded out the first inspiring idea—booted it into irretrievable oblivion, actually—and Average American punched the accelerator, making his way posthaste to the drive-through at the Ice Cream Palace.

Fact: 78 percent of Americans don't reach daily recommended activity levels.

"WelcometoIceCreamPa-a-a-a-lace!" the excited high schooler shouted from the speaker. "WhhaatkinIgitya?"

"Um."

Average American thought for a moment. But he already knew what he was going to order. "Could I have one of those cherry-covered, cream-topped, banana sundaes with chocolate, vanilla, and strawberry ice cream with extra nuts?"

"Andhows'boutsumsprinklesontop?" the voice offered.

For a full ten seconds, Average American's willpower fought a mortal battle against his sugar-conditioned cravings. Finally he gasped, "No, thank you."

Another victory!

Fact: The number of overweight Americans has doubled since 1980. And for adolescents, it's tripled.

"That'llbeee...$3.58atthefirstwindow!" shouted the Ice Cream Palace worker. "Please drive through!"

Average American paid for and took the cherry-covered, cream-topped, banana sundae with chocolate, vanilla, and strawberry ice cream with extra nuts and drove back the way he had come, skillfully eating as he drove. This time, he took no notice when he passed the Feel Healthy Gym.

Fact: Obesity is second only to smoking as the leading cause of preventable death. And if trends continue, obesity will soon be number one.

Later that afternoon, Average American experienced utter bewilderment as he collapsed from a heart attack. He was fifty-two.

56

STAYING ALIVE FOR GOD

To fulfill my Chazown—God's vision for every aspect of my life—staying in good physical shape is incredibly important. There's no way I could accomplish all the facets of my Chazown if my body were to let me down.

The same is true for you. As God reveals His purpose for your life to you, if you're going to realize your potential impact, you need to maintain a physical condition that honors Him and allows you to energetically pursue His vision for your life.

Paul wrote, "Do you not know that your body is a temple of the Holy Spirit, who is in you, whom you have received from God? You are not your own; you were bought at a price. Therefore honor God with your body" (1 Corinthians 6:19–20). The context of this passage deals with sexual purity. But consider the implications of the basic fact that, if you are a Christian, the Spirit of God resides in you.

How do you want to keep house for God?

> KEY THOUGHT
> *Every body ends up somewhere. But few bodies end up somewhere on purpose.*

You might say, "I serve a big God; that's why I have a big body." Sorry. That's probably an excuse to avoid facing the truth (you want to serve God but you hate self-discipline).

The night before Jesus was crucified, He asked His disciples to stay awake and pray with Him. Their bodies were tired; He was asking for physical discipline. When He found them asleep, He said, "Watch and pray so that you will not fall into temptation. The spirit is willing, but the body is weak" (Mark

14:38). There are times when the inclinations of our bodies run contrary to God's assignments. That's why we must go to God for strength in those areas of eating and exercise that determine our level of fitness.

Maybe you can relate to Paul's struggle. "I do not understand what I do. For what I want to do I do not do, but what I hate I do" (Romans 7:15). Many would say it this way today: *The things I know I shouldn't eat, I end up eating; and the things I know I should eat, I don't.* The same would go for exercise, eating and drinking habits, rest, sleep, substance abuse, stress management, and many other issues that directly impact our physical health.

K EY THOUGHT
Where there is no vision for our physical health, our bodies get out of control and fail us.

Maybe you identify with Paul's cry: "Who will rescue me from this body of death?" (verse 24).

His answer? Only God (see verse 25).

Scripture makes it clear that caring for our bodies is not just important physically—it's important spiritually. God has made us managers—not owners—over all our possessions, including our bodies and our physical lives. He expects us to care well for His property. In the same way that it's not "spiritual" to teach Sunday school while being routinely careless about finances, you and I are not fully serving God when we love God in our hearts but neglect Him in our bodies. He wants us to surrender our whole beings to Him.

> Scripture makes it clear that caring for our bodies is not just important physically—it's important spiritually. God has made us managers—not owners—over all our possessions, including our bodies.

And He's always right there to help us with the maintenance plan.

57

MYOPIC ME-MANAGEMENT

Self-discipline is especially difficult in our culture. Why? *Because most fail to see the cause-effect nature of life.* We suffer from shortsightedness.

This is especially true when it comes to our physical bodies.

Suntan today. Skin cancer tomorrow.

Beer party today. Beer belly tomorrow.

Supersize meal today. Supersize body tomorrow.

Sexual promiscuity today. Sexually transmitted disease, unwanted pregnancy, and emotional heartbreak tomorrow…

You see where I'm going.

Someone said, "Discipline is doing what I *can* do today, to enable me to do tomorrow what I *can't* do today."

> "Discipline is doing what I can do today, to enable me to do tomorrow what I can't do today."

Can you lower your cholesterol ten points by bedtime? I doubt it.

Can you run a marathon if you haven't jogged in years? No way.

Can you lose ten pounds in a day? You shouldn't even try.

But you can do something. Decide to do something today to honor God with your body.

Put down the brownie. Take a vigorous walk. Do twenty sit-ups. Read a book on dieting.

You'll be relieved to know—if you don't already—that what God asks of you physically is *not* the same thing as what all the Hollywood, media, and marketing messages seem to say. God made you to be *you*, not some alien body type or version of perfection now appearing at a theater near you. But that doesn't mean God doesn't care deeply about your good health, your physical stewardship of His gracious gifts to you, the beautiful best that He sees when He sees you.

What are you waiting for? A pill? An easy lie?

Why not make a plan that will put you further ahead tomorrow than you are today. Then repeat your plan the next day, and the next, and the next until your life is defined, not by where you are on any one day, but by the very promising direction you're headed.

> What are you waiting for?
> A pill? An easy lie?

You know that a small choice can have huge consequences...eventually. So just begin. Choose now.

What are you waiting for?

58

CHAZOWN IN THE KITCHEN

As with any fundamental priority in your life, your physical health requires vision into the future. So let me help you set your sights down the road to scope out God's chazown for your physical health.

I have a pair of "binoculars" you can borrow. (But I need them back by next Wednesday.) The two "lenses" of these binoculars are two important questions. And both questions come from Paul's words: "No one ever hated his own body, but he *feeds* and *cares for* it, just as Christ does the church" (Ephesians 5:29).

The first question is, *How will you feed your body? Are you honoring God in the way you eat?*

We talked earlier about the inner battle between our natural, fleshly tendencies and God's desires for us. When it comes to your diet, the battle is between two people living inside you: Fat Guy and Lean Guy. Fat Guy wants to eat everything; Lean Guy is more picky, more health conscious. Every time you're faced with the opportunity to put something in your mouth, these two combatants wage war inside you.

Which one are you going to listen to?

You can find hundreds of books on various diets, and many work well. But your body is unique. And the diet that works for one might not work for you. That's why you need guidance from a knowledgeable friend, a doctor, or a physical trainer about what's best for you. Then try one. Give it time, so you can see if it's right for you. If not, try something else.

And use common sense. For example, eat smaller portions. In our home, Amy uses smaller plates; we load up once, and that's it. Also, choose healthy alternatives—grilled instead of fried, fruit or vegetables instead of chips, water instead of soft drinks.

Bottom line: While you're seeking new ideas, use the knowledge you already have about nutrition. You're smart. Why not live smart and eat smart?

John Maxwell is one of my favorite teachers on leadership. In one book he shared that he was gaining more weight than was healthy, and he began to experience heart problems. His doctor told him he was facing a life-and-death decision.

Maxwell was known for his love for desserts. After beginning his new diet, he refused dessert at a dinner. Someone asked, "John, have you lost your craving for dessert?" Maxwell answered, "No, my craving for life outweighs my craving for dessert."[16]

> You're smart. Why not live smart and eat smart?

What is God trying to tell you about your treatment of the body He loaned you? Seek Him and listen. He may be speaking through your friends, through your doctor, through your conscience. Aggressively establish a plan of action, and begin honoring God in the way you eat.

59

EVERY BODY NEEDS A LITTLE LOVE

As we saw in the preceding chapter, Paul wrote, "No one ever hated his own body, but he feeds and *cares for* it" (Ephesians 5:29). So my second question about your physical health is, *How will you care for your body?*

Think about it. If I loaned you a book, I trust you'd keep it out of the rain. If you borrowed my car, I believe you wouldn't take it drag racing. (My Suburban would lose anyway.)

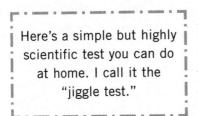

Here's a simple but highly scientific test you can do at home. I call it the "jiggle test."

Why would I hold these expectations? Because I trust you would care for what is mine. And that is one reason that caring for your body is so important. It is God's. Not yours.

I suggest three ways to care for your body. The first is *routine checkups.* There is nothing unspiritual about seeking guidance from those gifted and trained in the science of the body's workings. In fact, it's great stewardship.

So go see your dentist twice a year. Get your annual physical. Especially if you think something might be wrong. When my previous assistant, Sarah, was twenty-six, she found a lump on her body. Others said, "Don't worry. You're only twenty-six." But the reason she doesn't have cancer today is that she got it checked and removed by a pro.

The second way to care for your body is *consistent exercise.* How do you know if you need to exercise more?

Do you find that you are winded walking up a flight of stairs? Are you always tired? Do you find it difficult to get out of bed in the morning? Has the snooze button become your best friend?

Here's a simple but highly scientific test you can do at home. I call it the "jiggle test." Strip naked and stand in front of a mirror. Have a stopwatch handy. Lift your right foot and slam it down. At the same time, start your stopwatch. If you're still jiggling after thirty seconds, get to the gym. *Today.*

Yes, I know. When the alarm goes off at 6:00 a.m. for you to go jogging, Fat Guy says, "Go back to sleep." Take his pudgy face and put duct tape across his mouth. Don't listen to him.

But, Craig, I don't have time to exercise.

News flash! You will make time for whatever you believe is a priority. It's a fact. You prove it every day. Face it.

When my assistant started, I told her part of her job was to guard at least three workouts a week in my schedule. Why? It is a priority.

If you're just getting started, choose a small, reasonable goal. Set yourself up for victory. Create a habit of consistently doing whatever will take you to the next step of physical discipline.

The third way to care for your body is to *face crippling addictions...and do what's necessary to overcome them.* When Paul wrote to the believers at Corinth, he confronted an attitude that was, to use some of today's terms, *progressive, tolerant, open-minded.* In 1 Corinthians 6:12, he quoted someone who made the excuse: "Everything is permissible for me." Then Paul answered, "But not everything is beneficial." Someone else justified himself: "Everything is permissible for me." Paul answered, "But I will not be mastered by anything."

> "I can quit anytime," you've said. Then why haven't you? You cannot overcome what you are willing to tolerate.

What has mastered you? What's in control of your life? What destructive behavior at this moment seems bigger and stronger than you? *That* is the definition of an addiction.

Maybe you're in denial. What do other people say has mastered you?

"I can quit anytime," you've said. Then why haven't you?

You cannot overcome what you are willing to tolerate.

Most of us are aware of obvious addictions—smoking, alcohol, drugs (including prescription medications). But for many it's food or caffeine or video games or sexual sin.

If anything other than God is mastering you, you cannot fully fulfill your Chazown. You and God must defeat all usurpers to His throne. If you are in bondage to tobacco, you will weaken your lungs, your life span, and potentially your witness. If you are hooked on pornography, you may appear normal, but inside your heart is shriveling in sin. If something besides God has you in its grip, act now. Ask God to help you move toward freedom. And start walking.

60

"PROPERTY OF GOD"

Tommy Lasorda, a Los Angeles Dodgers baseball icon, admitted to a problem with smoking. So he looked at his cigarettes and asked himself, "Who is stronger? You or me?" He found it within his power to say, "I'm stronger," and he put them down and quit. Then he looked at his drink and asked the alcohol, "Who is stronger? You or me?" Again, he came out on top and quit drinking. Finally he looked at his linguine with clam sauce and asked, "Who is stronger? You or me?" The little clam answered back from his plate, "I am." So he decided he couldn't conquer linguine with clam sauce.[17]

You, on the other hand, can defeat anything because you have the power of God living inside you. Even if you've tried one hundred times unsuccessfully, with God's power you can succeed the hundred-and-first time.

And gather supportive people who will pray for you, challenge you, encourage you, provide you with resources, celebrate your victories, and help you up when you fall. With God's power, expressed through His people, you can defeat anything.

> Remember...your body is stamped "Property of God." It's been purchased by the blood of Christ.

A guy at church asked me to pray that he would stop smoking. He tried to win this battle for years but was losing. We prayed. The next day, he won the battle. He won again the second day and the third. When I saw him a week later, he shouted, "Pastor Craig, I've been free for seven days!" In another week, he told me it had been fourteen days. For over a year, he has been giving me the weekly count. You can do it too.

Remember…your body is stamped "Property of God." It's been purchased by the blood of Christ.

How will you feed your body? How will you care for your body? How will you honor God with this amazing, intricate instrument He's placed in your care for the fulfillment of His dream?

YOU'RE THE AUTHOR

Your Health and Fitness

Give careful, prayerful thought to answering the following questions. Then, if you're not sure where to start in writing goals and action steps, pick the top one in each category that most resonates with your heart.

HOW WILL YOU FEED YOUR BODY?

- Do you need to eliminate certain foods from your diet?
- Do you need to eat healthy snacks rather than junk food?
- In what area(s) of eating do you lack discipline?
- Should you take a permanent fast from fast food?
- Should you eliminate the wrong drinks (coffee, lattes, soft drinks, alcohol) and replace them with water?
- Do you need supplemental vitamins or other nutrients?
- What question are you secretly relieved that I haven't asked? (Ask it.)

HOW WILL YOU CARE FOR YOUR BODY?

- Do you need a physical or some other sort of doctor's examination?
- Do you need to begin regular exercise?
- Are you addicted to something that you need to overcome? (Be honest.)
- Do you need more sleep?
- Are you living with stress? Do you need to find appropriate relief?
- Are you taking adequate time off?
- Are you a workaholic?
- What question are you secretly relieved that I haven't asked? (Ask it.)

SHORT-TERM GOALS

Now define one or two specific health and fitness goals based on your previous selections. Make sure each goal is achievable and measurable.

VERY NEXT STEP

Now describe the specific action you'll take to realize your chosen goals. Provide plans, time frames, specific actions—whatever it will take for you to follow through.

What do you want to do next? If you're ready to continue and create an action plan in another life area, then read on.

But maybe you want to take the goals you've already established and live them out for a while before considering action plans in other areas. If that's the case, it's important for you to read the last part of the book. Please skip ahead to page 193, and finish reading the book from that point.

For more resources, visit www.chazown.com.

WORK

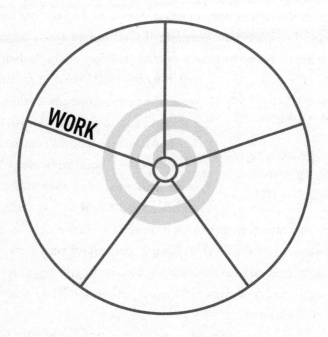

61

GETTING TO WHY

L ife is filled with important questions. For example, why do they make lemonade with artificial lemon flavoring but dishwashing detergent with real lemons? Why isn't *phonics* spelled the way it sounds? And why do you press harder on the remote control when you know the batteries are dead?

Here's another important question: If God put everyone on earth for a reason, why are so many men and women trudging through their workday watching the clock, waiting for the day, the week, the year—an entire working life—to end? And end so they can do what? Die of a heart attack three months after retirement?

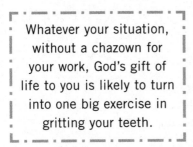

Whatever your situation, without a chazown for your work, God's gift of life to you is likely to turn into one big exercise in gritting your teeth.

Of course, your work doesn't have to come with a paycheck to qualify as your oc-cupation. You might be a student, a stay-at-home mom, or a volunteer at church or in the community.

But whatever your situation, without a chazown for your work, God's gift of life to you is likely to turn into one big exercise in gritting your teeth.

So how do you know what God wants you to do? That's what I want to talk about in this section.

First, to clarify: Your *life's work* is to pursue your Chazown for God's glory as a fully devoted follower of Jesus Christ. But here, I'm focusing on your *work life*. Depending on your circumstances today, the two terms might be almost the same thing. For example, if you know your Chazown and you're already fully pursuing it, then you're hard at work at your life's work!

But for many—and all of us at different seasons—our work life is differ-ent and less. Our work life is what we're occupied with now to earn our keep.

It's our job, our nine-to-five commitment. That obligation might be getting us closer to our Chazown, or it might not. But whatever it is, that obligation is our work.

In a way, our work life is where many of the concepts we've been examining come together. There's just no getting around the fact that our work is often the place where all the other areas converge to shape our reason for being on earth. As I've just indicated, for many, your God-ordained work is the task for which He created you.

Unfortunately, many people I meet are in the dark about work. Some have been raised in families where little or nothing was expected of them, or where the value of work with dignity was not modeled. Some struggle to find the right questions, or are smart enough to sniff out the wrong ones (like, *What can I do to earn the most money with the least effort?*).

Some are just stuck.

The result is that millions end up just punching a clock—literally or figuratively—until their time is up and they rest easy in that final bed.

Do you have a clear sense of what you were created and gifted to do? Or why you're doing what you're doing on the job?

When you don't know the reason for a thing's existence, it's hard to avoid misusing it. When I was six, my seven-year-old neighbor, Ashley, came over to play. She found a plastic triangle-shaped thing with holes in it on the ground. She guessed it was an oxygen mask, so she put it to her face and started breathing through it. If she had known it was an athletic cup and had known its purpose, she wouldn't have put it to such an inappropriate use. (Gross, huh?)

If you don't know your purpose—the reason why you're here—you'll misuse your life, missing God's best!

So who knows the purpose of a person? *The Manufacturer.*

If you want to put your life to its best, most fulfilling use, begin by asking the One who made you. Ask patiently, humbly, and sincerely. Keep asking. (Recognize a theme in *Chazown* by now?) Be sure to listen to what your loving Creator and His people tell you.

And when you're ready, turn the page.

62

LABOR'S LOVE LOST

Everyone works. Not everyone gets a paycheck for what they do, but everyone works.

My definition of *work* is whatever you do with your productive, waking hours. For example, my wife, Amy, does the hardest job; she makes our home a great place for our kids to grow into fully devoted followers of Christ. That's her work. If you're a student, then school is your work. If you volunteer at a library, that's work.

Since most of what you do is your work, God's chazown for your work life is vitally important.

KEY THOUGHT
Where there is no vision for your work life, you will mostly work at wasting time.

Without a dream, a revelation from God, you simply toil day in and day out, filling the empty hours in a passionless, purposeless, plain-vanilla existence. You get up, go to work, come home, go to bed. Then you do it all over again.

> Everyone works. Not everyone gets a paycheck for what they do, but everyone works.

So what's it like when you do the default thing, laboring without divinely determined direction? The clock becomes your enemy.

Solomon captured it: "I hated life, because the work that is done under the sun was grievous to me. All of it is meaningless, a chasing after the wind" (Ecclesiastes 2:17). Does that resonate with you? You're working forty or fifty hours a week, and it's *grievous* to you? You're not maximizing the gifts God has given you? Your work has little or nothing to do with your core values? You're merely passing time for a paycheck?

Can you say you love your job? Or are you in an occupation that doesn't light your fire?

It's okay. You can be honest. I won't tell your boss.

If so, cheer up! You can become one of the few who works according to your chazown from God, so your work will end up somewhere on purpose.

The Bible says that you "are God's workmanship, created in Christ Jesus to do good works, which God prepared in advance for us to do" (Ephesians 2:10). Before the first humans existed, God looked forward to you, and He skillfully custom-designed your unique blueprint. You are His workmanship. He knew exactly what He was doing when He created you.

God established a purpose for your life, to fulfill His Chazown for you. He wrote out a celestial to-do list just for you. He selected certain people for you to meet and influence and love, certain world-impacting tasks for you to perform.

K EY THOUGHT
All work ends up somewhere—but few people's work ends up somewhere on purpose.

What's more, the way God designed you and the works He prepared for you—the two correspond perfectly. He wired you and gifted you to fulfill His divine assignments. When you're doing the tasks God placed you here to do, there's nothing else you'd rather be doing.

I'll be the first to say that one person's meaningful work can be another's meaningless torture.

Most of us have known a high school janitor who influenced scores of young lives with her ready smile and words of wisdom.

Or a lifelong millworker whose example of integrity and responsibility made him the hero to a houseful of sons.

Or the mom who never finished her education but raised up a family whose influence for God is still ringing down through the generations.

Or the CEO who realized he was miserable making huge bonuses but deeply happy rolling up his sleeves for peanuts in a Third World mission.

So I don't want to make any careless assumptions. But my passion is to help those hundreds of young men and women I've talked to in my lifetime who are afraid that God has no first-best for their work life…and they're about to give up the search.

Are you one? Are you bone tired of "chasing after wind"?

I promise you that when you get to spend forty or fifty hours a week fulfilling God's chazown in your work, you'll never describe your life as "grievous" or "meaningless." Those words will drop to the bottom of your vocabulary list, and "passionate," "excited," and "meaningful" will be at the top.

> When you do the default thing, laboring without divinely determined direction, the clock becomes your enemy.

What is your vision for your work five years from now? Ten years from now?

Where there is no vision, you're likely to feel so bored or frustrated or depressed you'll wish you could perish.

63

THE LADDER
AT THE TOP OF EVEREST

Question: For this season of your life, are you doing the work God wants you to do?

In other words, are you maxing out the gifts He has given you, hitting the bull's-eye of your core values, putting into tangible action the passion that burns in your heart?

Yes or no?

If your answer is yes, that's fantastic! Let me offer you two suggestions. *Celebrate and elevate.*

First, celebrate. Why? Because you're living the dream.

Stop and enjoy the moment. Worship God. He's given you His Chazown, and you've responded faithfully.

When Amy and I were in the hospital, welcoming our sixth child, our doctor—a close friend named Dr. Kelly Stephens—came to visit. In our conversation, he brought up my teaching about Chazown and said, "Craig, I love this stuff about discovering God's dream. But what if I'm already living it?"

"Kelly," I answered, "you celebrate. Because not many people have what you have." This man is doing precisely what God prepared in advance for him to do.

When this happens, enjoy it! Embrace it! Have a party with God!

And second, elevate. Take your work to the next level.

Don't settle in as though you've arrived. If you're doing what God has uniquely created you to do, then ask Him what's next.

Several years ago, when our church filled in four worship experiences each week, it would have been easy for me to tell myself, *Hey! God helped me build a church. It's healthy. Now I'm going to consolidate my gains. Sit back and enjoy the reward of a job well done.*

But God led me to think outside the box. *I wonder if it's possible we're just getting started. Is it possible...just possible, God, that You really do want us to really, You know...go into all the world? Instead of building a church and asking people to come to us, maybe we could take the church to them. Maybe we can expand this very same church into a second campus. Maybe a third.*

> Is there some ceiling that all the experts say cannot be surpassed? Do you dare to dream that God is big enough to help you break through it?

And suddenly God elevated His work to the next level.

Now we refuse to believe we'll ever see the end of what He can do through our ministry.

If you're currently doing what God wants you to do, ask Him, *What's next?* Can you possibly work more efficiently, making a greater profit so that you can contribute more? Is there some ceiling that all the experts say cannot be surpassed? Do you dare to dream that God is big enough to help you break through it?

Celebrate and elevate.

Say, *God, thank You.* Then ask, *God, where should we go from here?*

Yes, you've arrived. You're at Base Camp One. Great job!

Rope up with God, and climb on!

MEANING IN THE MUNDANE

B ut what if your answer is no?

What should you do if you honestly say, "For this season of life, I'm *not* doing the work that God wants me to do. I know there's something more. Something different. I know my life's work can have greater significance than it does now."

If your answer is no, I have two things to say.

First, *don't panic.*

God is still in control. You may not see it, but He is still working in your life, guiding you toward the place where you will make your greatest contribution. And if you've been resisting Him, sprinting down the wrong road, turn around now. He'll guide you where you need to go.

Second, *trust God.*

Hear God's promise in Proverbs 3:5–6, and let these words be life to you: "Trust in the LORD with all your heart and lean not on your own understanding; in all your ways acknowledge him, and he will make your paths straight."

When you drag yourself out of bed and make the same old commute to a frustrating, dead-end job—trust God. When you're working with people you'd rather punch than love—trust God. When you've seen your dream, and you believe it's God's dream for you, but at the moment you're in the wrong place, doing the wrong work—even there, acknowledge God in all your ways. Trust Him, and He will make your paths straight.

Don't panic. Trust God.

Think about David, before he was King David. When he was still a kid— very likely a young teenager—God guided the prophet Samuel to anoint David the next king of Israel. God essentially told young David, "You are My workmanship, created to do good works I prepared even before you were born. You will lead My people."

David knew his Chazown.

So how did he spend the next several years of his life? Circling in a holding pattern. God was preparing him. David continued to lead sheep, which, it turns out, are as hard to lead as people. He learned to fight, fending off wild animals to protect his flock. He learned the value of a quiet, contemplative retreat, growing ever closer to the heart of God. He spent hours on the harp and lyre, honing his gift for modeling and leading worship.

Even after King Saul admitted that David would be Israel's next king, David spent years in exile, on the run, living in caves.

David could have said, "I might as well give up. I'll never get to do what I was created to do."

But he didn't panic. He trusted God.

If you're crossing the same kind of emotional desert, then you do the same.

Right out of college I knew my Chazown. I felt so called to ministry I couldn't see straight. I would have worked for free.

But nobody wanted me then.

So I took a job in another direction—in the business world—selling burglar alarms door-to-door. *Knock, knock, knock.* "Good morning, ma'am. If I could just have a few minutes of your time…"

For me, door-to-door sales was at the bottom of the business-world food chain. I hated every minute of it.

But what was God doing? He was teaching me to submit to authority. He was teaching me to handle rejection. He taught me relational skills. He showed me how to reach out to those who weren't at first interested in what I had to offer.

Great lessons for ministry.

I knew what God had called me to do. But I didn't realize the education I needed first.

He was preparing me.

Maybe He's preparing you.

YOU'RE THE AUTHOR

Your Work

So you're asking, *How do I know God's chazown for my work life?*

Good question. Glad you asked. Take a deep breath, and prepare to take a long, hard look at all your thoughts and conclusions so far. As I've already mentioned, understanding God's chazown for your work life is often at the very heart of His plan for the rest of your life too.

Your Own Chazown. Begin by looking over the notes you've written in your Chazown journal. What are the common themes? What causes you to salivate? What lures and entices your whole inner being toward making an impact for God, toward living well for eternity?

Look again at the Three Circles that are so helpful in revealing our personal Chazown:

1. What are your *core values*? What's burning deep within you, threatening to burst out into reality?
2. What are your *spiritual gifts*? What are you sickeningly good at?
3. What are your formative *past experiences*? Those events, both pleasant and painful, that God has used to prepare you for your Chazown?

Your Purpose Statement. You've already written a tentative purpose statement based on these questions. Review that statement, and ask God for further insight to understand how all of the pieces of your life fit together. As He provides His vision, write down your thoughts.

Two Revealing Questions. Consider again the two questions we discussed earlier:

> **Question #1:** If money were no object and you could do anything you wanted for the rest of your life, what would you do?

Question #2: Besides ministering to those who are most important to you, what is the number one thing that you believe God wants to accomplish through you?

I'm talking about something really important. Something that will last forever. Dream big.

As you look inward for the answers, also look upward. Persistently ask God for guidance, and He will provide it. Write any new thoughts that come to mind about God's Chazown for you.

If you're seeing more clearly than ever that the work you're doing is your life's work (living out your Chazown), then—say it with me—celebrate and elevate.

Goals for Work. After you've celebrated, in order to elevate to the next step of God's vision, write one or two new, specific goals for your work. What can you do to impact more lives? To impact the same lives in a new way? To do your work more efficiently or effectively? To break into a whole new world of influence for eternity?

SHORT-TERM GOALS

Now define one or two specific work-life goals based on your previous answers. Make sure each goal is achievable and measurable.

VERY NEXT STEP

Now describe the specific action you will take to realize your chosen goals. Provide plans, time frames, specific actions—whatever it will take for you to follow through.

Goals for Change. On the other hand, if you aren't living your Chazown—if you realize you've been running the wrong way, or maybe you've done everything right, but your life feels wrong—*don't panic. Trust God.*

Trust is active, not passive. So write down one or two attainable goals that will move you toward the chazown in your work life that God is revealing to you. A book or a class? An interview? Gaining more experience? Researching options?

Attitude Check. One more thought from God to you: From this moment on, for the rest of your life—whether you're riding the long, slow, torturous climb up the back side of the roller coaster or you're flying down the exhilarating plunge toward your dreams, whether you're sweeping floors or sweeping souls by the thousands into the kingdom of God—keep one central, all-encompassing command in mind:

> Whatever you do, work at it with all your heart, as working for the Lord, not for men. (Colossians 3:23)

Whatever you are doing at this moment, do it for Him. With the best attitude He can give you. With everything in you.

Don't hold back.

For more resources, visit www.chazown.com.

PART 5

FROM HERE TO ETERNITY

Why you can't realize your Chazown alone

65

A NEW VIEW OF YOU

Congratulations. You've made significant progress. Surely God is pleased with you.

Let's review the road we've traveled so far and celebrate for a moment what God has shown us.

You decided that an accidental life was not for you. By seeking God's direction, His Chazown that was custom-designed for you, you will certainly end up somewhere on purpose.

Great decision.

You've explored your Three Circles. You can define your core values, your gifts, and your past experiences. Prayerfully, you have examined how these overlap and point toward God's Chazown for your life.

> You decided that an accidental life was not for you. You will certainly end up somewhere on purpose.

Another big step in God's direction.

You've narrowed the vision into one life-directing statement, and you have established specific, measurable, and written goals. With each step along the way, you have listed the next thing you need to do.

Excellent work.

You've decided to live fully committed to God, strengthening five priority areas (they're like spokes in a wheel that make winning your life's race possible). Your little c's are in place. You will please God in your relationship with Him, your relationships with people, your financial life, your physical life, and your work life.

God is pleased.

You are well on your way to living life according to God's best for you. You should feel great. But whatever you do, don't close the book just yet. We're not quite done.

We have one more unbelievably important concept to apply. It's summed up in a single word. But I should warn you.

The word is not popular.

And let me warn you about something else.

The word, and what it stands for, is not optional either. Not if you want to turn your new vision for your life into a reality for God.

HAZARDS AHEAD

W hat is the word? Before I tell you what it is, let me tell you why this key word is so important.

Because as much as God wants you to fulfill His destiny for your life, your spiritual enemy wants the exact opposite. The Evil One takes great delight in a wasted, directionless, self-honoring, God-ignoring life. And every force from hell will try to stop you from living your God-given Chazown.

May I be blunt?

You will face obstacles, mountains, and hurdles. You'll get distracted. You'll be tempted to wander off the road. You will procrastinate, putting off God's best for another day.

You will feel the irresistible pull of powerful idols: Materialism. Fame. Greed. Pleasure. Comfort. Applause. You will get tired, frustrated, and depressed. At times you'll want to quit.

You will experience dry times. Seasons when God seems far away or nonexistent. Bad habits will creep in. Sin will sneak up on you. Apathy will set in.

You'll face giants of doubt. Dragons of fear. Monsters of complacency.

One month you'll make major progress. The next month you will experience nothing but dramatic setbacks. Sometimes you'll question what, if anything, God has accomplished to date.

Was God really directing me? Is this what He really wanted for me? I'm not sure.

And then you can easily slip into defeat. *I can't do it,* you'll say. *This whole Chazown thing is stupid. Maybe I should just give it up.*

And that is why my final *word* to you is so important.

Accountability.

WE'RE ALL IN SCHOOL

Two things bothered me when I was in school.

The first was the teacher's ultimate weapon. You probably remember the piercing glare, the sinister smile as the teacher crooned with deceptive sweetness, "If you don't shape up, this will go on your...*permanent record.*" Even today, just seeing those two words in print makes me break out in a cold sweat.

The second thing that bothered me about school was—*gasp! (sounds of hyperventilating)...*

> If it was graded, then I'd want to put more effort into it.

I'm sorry, I still start to panic when I think of it. I'm talking about...well, you know...

Report card day. (Whew! There. I said it.)

That's why I was always asking, "Are we going to be graded on this?" Because if the work wasn't graded, then it didn't have any effect on the report card. *So let's party! Who cares?*

But if it was graded, then I'd want to put more effort into it.

Quite frankly, I liked it better when I wasn't graded.

Little did I understand that school was preparing me for life.

In life we are creating a permanent record by the way we live.

And yes, everything will be graded. It all goes into the final report card.

Or, to put it the way the Bible does, God will call every one of us to give account for all that we've done with our lives. "Nothing in all creation is hidden from God's sight. Everything is uncovered and laid bare before the eyes of him to whom we must give account" (Hebrews 4:13).[18]

You thought Mrs. Snerdblat in the fifth grade had eyes in the back of her head? You couldn't get away with anything? Well, she was an amateur compared to God. He sees everything.

And it's good for us that He does. Whether you realized it or not, Mrs. Snerdblat's intention was to help you become a person of wisdom and integrity. God's motive is the same. He loves us, and He knows we will find the greatest fulfillment when we pursue and fulfill our Chazown. That's why He warns us ahead of time, "You're creating a permanent record. And everything will be on the final exam." He's motivating us to live for our own best interest.

> To put it the way the Bible does, God will call every one of us to give account for all that we've done with our lives.

The greatest dream of any Christ-follower is to stand one day before God and hear Him say, "Well done."

Is that your dream? Then the best way to ensure you will hear "well done" when you give account to God is by giving account first to other followers of Christ here and now.

That's why the phrase "hold me accountable" must be part of our everyday vocabulary.

Stop and practice it now. Say, "Hold me accountable."

Good. Now smile and explain to the person in the bus seat next to you that you always talk to yourself.

68

MOVED BY ACCOUNTABILITY

On Sunday, January 9, 2005, I was sharing a chazown for our church to launch a new campus in the fall. But we were unsure where the new location would be. Nonetheless, I dared to suggest that at least one hundred people prepare to pack their bags and be sent out to start the new campus—wherever they might be—in order to reach people for Christ.

A short time later, one of our executive assistants, Sherri, took a phone call.

"Hello, this is Sherri. How can I help you?"

"Hi, Sherri, my name is Cari. My husband, Kevin, and I have been praying, and we believe God is calling us to move and help start the new campus. We are supposed to be part of the hundred people. We believe this is our Chazown."

> Accountability makes the difference between what you say you want to do and what you actually do.

This was no small undertaking for them, a family with two children. This brave couple had been married for seventeen years and never lived outside Oklahoma. All their family lived close by. Kevin had a big law practice he would have to leave behind. They had absolutely no reason to leave, except that God was calling them.

Sherri, catching her breath, responded, "Wow, that's awesome!"

Cari explained how God had prepared them for this moment. "We are passionate about evangelism, and we would die for what God is doing through our church. Our experience starting the law practice has uniquely prepared us to help start this campus. Our gifts, values, and experiences completely match the need. We have sought God and know this is what He's calling us to do."

Then, her voice still shaky, Cari said, "But we're afraid that when we find out where it is...we might back out." She then uttered the words that sealed her commitment before God. "Sherri, will you hold us accountable to move?"

Many of us have great intentions, but our follow-through often leaves much to be desired. It's human nature. That's why God put us together in a family.

K EY THOUGHT
Accountability closes the gap between intentions and actions.

You can never fulfill your Chazown without accountability, because...

Accountability makes the difference between what you *say* you want to do and what you *actually do*. Without it, God's dream for your life will always remain a dream.

On the first weekend of April, we announced the location of the new campus: Phoenix, Arizona.

Cari and Kevin, with dozens of other people, packed their bags and moved.

69

DIFFERENT KINDS OF DROPOUTS

Let's face it. A lot of us don't like to be held accountable. We push it away. Why? Let me introduce you to four people, each of whom would give you a different answer to that question.

First, meet Fearful Freddy. Since childhood, Freddy's been paralyzed at the thought of failure. While others tried new things and began new adventures, Freddy remained safely behind. Freddy was loaded with talent, full of hopes and dreams. But his dreams never came to pass. *What if I fail?* he always asked himself.

Freddy never played a sport or an instrument. He never went to the dance or ran for class secretary. He was afraid to interview for the job he really wanted or to volunteer at church.

Freddy never told anyone his dreams. If he did, he might have had to act on them. And who knew what might happen then? So he ran from accountability.

Eventually all of his dreams died. They drowned in fear.

Most of us, at some time or other, are plagued by questions like, *What if I don't measure up? What if I'm not good enough? What if I don't make the cut?*

We fear failure fiercely.

Next, I'd like to introduce you to Apathetic Allie. This bright young lady doesn't care about much—especially deep, committed, authentic relation-ships. It's not that she's antisocial; she just can't be bothered to go out of her way for a friend.

In reality, Allie's apathy is rooted in past relational wounds. She doesn't want to risk vulnerability, so she *chooses* not to care. *What good have people ever done me? My parents neglected me. My high school friends hurt me. People at work are two-faced and only out for themselves. Church people are hypocrites. Why should I bother being close to anyone?*

So Allie mostly goes through life alone.

Do you find yourself avoiding accountability, justifying yourself with questions like, *What does it matter? Who cares? Is this really going to help me?*

Third, there's Rebellious Ricky. Even as a child, Ricky hated rules. His parents hoped he'd outgrow his rebellious attitude. He never did.

In grade school, if the teacher said to walk, Ricky would run. If everyone else dressed up, Ricky wore jeans. If the speed limit was sixty-five, Ricky would exceed eighty—often drunk.

As you can see, Ricky is rebellious. That's why he resists accountability. *I don't answer to anybody. If you try to tell me what to do, I'll do the opposite. Who are you to butt into my life? I'll do whatever I want.*

Ring any bells?

And finally, I'd like you to meet Prideful Polly. Polly believes she knows best. Everyone else is either wrong or in her way. Her life's motto? "If you want something done right, you have to do it yourself." She refuses advice and shuns assistance, even when she knows she needs it—*especially* when she knows she needs it.

> She refuses advice and shuns assistance, even when she knows she needs it—especially when she knows she needs it.

Polly puts on her best public front, but she limps through life.

Accountability? "Ha!" sneers Polly. "Accountability is for losers."

How often do you see the same independent streak coming out in yourself? *I can do it alone. I don't need anybody's help.*

Perhaps you know someone like Fearful Freddy, Apathetic Allie, Rebellious Ricky, or Prideful Polly. Most likely you recognize one or more of these exaggerated caricatures as an aspect of yourself.

But to experience God's best for us, we need other Christ-followers to support, encourage, and correct us. Holding us accountable.

70

FORK IN THE ROAD

You've come a long way.

But in spite of all the work you've done throughout the earlier steps in this book, you're now at a point of decision. Your choice here will determine whether you will bring all of the dreaming and planning to fruition. Here's where you decide whether to turn your intentions into action or just let them stay in the realm of nice ideas.

You're at a fork in life's path. You have two choices. You can go back to life the way it was, without a Chazown. Without a vision, a dream, a revelation. No passion, no plan, no direction, no motivation, no purpose. Perishing daily on the inside.

Or you can find people to hold you accountable. You can move into a life of purpose. A purpose for which you were uniquely created. A purpose that follows a path blazed long ago by God, just for you.

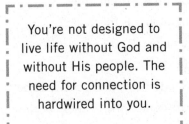

You're not designed to live life without God and without His people. The need for connection is hardwired into you.

At this juncture, please listen carefully: *You'll never do all that God wants you to do without His people holding you accountable.*

You're not designed to live life without God and without His people. The need for connection is hardwired into you. Walking life's path in good company is a prerequisite to reaching the destination of our dreams.

That's why, as we saw earlier, Solomon, the wisest man in history, wrote in Ecclesiastes 4:9–10, "Two are better than one, because they have a good return for their work: If one falls down, his friend can help him up. But pity the man who falls and has no one to help him up!" God says we need a buddy system.

If you're taking this walk alone and you fall, who will help you up—spiritually, emotionally, relationally…maybe even physically? Very few people can get back to their feet and continue with God's plan without personal accountability.

The signpost stands in front of you. Right now. At the fork in the road.

God and His people are a little way down one path, beckoning you to come with them to your destiny, your dream.

But you have four other companions coaxing you down the other path, back to life as it used to be. Their names are Fear, Apathy, Rebellion, and Pride. If you listen to them, you will walk alone.

> Their names are Fear, Apathy, Rebellion, and Pride. If you listen to them, you will walk alone.

Every day people choose that path. And people all around us are perishing.

You can't reach your Chazown alone.

TELL ME WHEN I'M WRONG

H ere are two thoughts from the Bible to help you understand even better why you desperately need others to help you along.

First, *you won't fulfill God's vision without correction.*

"We all, like sheep, have gone astray, each of us has turned to his own way" (Isaiah 53:6). Did you see the words *all* and *each* in that verse? Not a person alive today would consistently choose the right road without help. We all need someone who loves us enough to correct us when we drift the wrong way.

Have you ever driven a car whose front wheels are out of alignment? You have to keep pulling one direction on the steering wheel because the car keeps trying to stray off to the side of the road. It's bent, and it needs continual compensating pressure in the other direction.

We're bent too. We want to drive straight, but we keep pulling to the side.

When the gospel first came to Africa, some of the early converts became so passionate about prayer that they built their own private prayer huts. Each hut was set aside for just one person, and a path used only by that person led up to its door.

If someone neglected the loving discipline of prayer, guess what happened. Grass would begin to grow on his or her path.

The straying brother's or sister's best friends were those with the courage to say, "I love you, and I see there's grass growing on your path." In other words, *I love you enough to correct you. You're not doing what God has called you to do.*

Who loves you enough to point out the overgrown paths in your life?

You can't fulfill God's Chazown without correction.

Hold me accountable.

HELP ME WHEN I'M WEAK

Correction is not all you'll need. There's a second component to accountability.

You won't fulfill your Chazown without support.

Remember David? Anointed the next king of Israel?

He knew his Chazown many years before he assumed the throne. Throughout his many difficult experiences during that waiting period, David could have given up a hundred different times.

David's greatest trouble was the reigning king, Saul. He was jealous of David and kept trying to kill him.

But God knew what David needed to stay the course. He needed a friend for support. So God provided none other than Saul's own son, Jonathan.

Once when David was hiding in the desert, Jonathan went secretly to him and "helped him find strength in God" (1 Samuel 23:16).

One man helped another man find strength—not in self-determination, not in an army, not in positive thinking—but in God. That's an important part of what an accountability partner does.

Jonathan recognized God's choice of David as Israel's next king, and in his support of David he disobeyed his own father—who, to be honest, was a few megabytes short of a DVD. Jonathan said in essence, "David, I'll see to it that you fulfill your destiny."

I promise you, when you begin to understand your Chazown, Satan will do his best to talk you out of it. Few if any people have the perspective and stamina to continue climbing solo toward God's Chazown.

Who will support you? Who will help you to resist giving up?

Hold me accountable.

SURPRISE COMEBACK

I started playing tennis as a freshman in high school, which is typically too late to start tennis and expect to play competitively in college. My coach was Ken Ellinger. Against the odds, Ken believed I would play college tennis.

"Groeschel," he said, "we're going to do it."

He assumed the role of mentor in all areas of my life. And he worked me. And worked me.

And worked me.

In time, Ken helped me acquire a tennis scholarship with a top-ranked school.

And I was completely outclassed. The only reason they kept me was because I was their transportation. I had the only car. My first year, everyone on the team was winning big. Except me. I lost almost every time.

> I was completely out-classed. The only reason they kept me was because I was their transportation.

Knowing how I was struggling, Ken came to watch me play. And, as usual, all of my teammates won, and I lost. Not only did I lose; I got skunked: 6–0, 6–0.

That's when I decided to quit. I threw my equipment around, broke my racket, and said words that didn't make God proud. I ran off the court in tears. Back at my dorm room, I shouted that I was quitting for good.

And I meant it.

Ken followed me to my room. I sat pouting.

I'll never forget what he said.

He leaned back casually and said, "Well, Groeschel, I'm glad I got to be here today."

I wanted to tell him where he could go.

He continued, "I'm here on one of the most important days of your life. Because today is the day we'll see who you're going to become."

Then he leaned forward and looked me straight in the eye. "Today," he said, "you'll decide whether you're a quitter or a fighter. And I get to be here to see your decision.

"Groeschel, most people are quitters. They take the easy way out. And you'll probably do it too. Unless…unless deep inside you, you can find something I've believed was there from the first day we met. And if it's really there, then today you'll become a fighter.

"If you fight, you have to go back, suck it up, put your tail between your legs, and apologize to all those people. But if you're really a fighter, you'll be up to it."

> "Groeschel, most people are quitters. They take the easy way out. And you'll probably do it too. Unless…"

I'm so thankful he was there that day. He supported me. On that day I made a decision that sticks with me to this day. Because of Ken, I'm not a quitter. I'm a fighter. I fight, and I fight for the things that matter most.

It took two more years, but eventually I set a school record for the most consecutive wins. I was named athlete of the year on the team that finished fifth in the nation.

Why? Because one man loved me enough to support me when I needed it most.

LIVING FOR
THE SECOND EMBRACE

You've got one shot to make this life count. Live for what I call "the second embrace."

If you know Jesus Christ as Savior and Lord, one day you will enter heaven and stand before Him. He'll look at you with a genuine smile. In that moment, you'll know without a doubt you belong. You'll never again experience rejection or abandonment.

With warmth you can't imagine, He will embrace you and say, "Welcome home. From now on, forever, I share My kingdom with you."

> He'll look you in the eye. And He'll say, "Well done." All heaven will pause to listen. "Well done, My good and faithful servant."

But then He'll step back and examine your life's work—everything you did for Him. If He's pleased with it—and you might be surprised what will and won't please Him—He'll reach out His nail-pierced hands and grab you a second time. He'll look you in the eye.

And He'll say, "Well done." All heaven will pause to listen. "Well done, My good and faithful servant."

Everyone ends up somewhere.

We will end up somewhere on purpose.

YOU'RE THE AUTHOR

Your Accountability Plan

Are you a quitter or a fighter?

What's your decision? To settle for meaningless, directionless living? Or to forge ahead in God's strength toward your Chazown with the correction and support of others?

Think back on the dreams God has awakened within you. Dreams about your relationships with Him and with people. Dreams about your financial and physical health. And dreams about your life's work.

I know you want to succeed in all these. The first step might be a hard one to take: find one person who's loving enough and strong enough to help you take that step.

Today I have eleven people who hold me accountable in different areas. I'm challenging you to find just one.

If you're ready to rise to the challenge, pray this prayer (or put the same ideas into your own words) and sign it as your contractual commitment to God.

Dear God,

I commit to prayerfully find someone to hold me accountable to fulfill Your Chazown for my relationship with You, my relationships with other people, my physical life, my financial life, and my life's work. Please lead me to the right person. In Jesus' name,

Amen.

Signed _____

Date _____

Consider these proven pointers for life-changing accountability:

- **Meet regularly.** It could be a daily phone call, a weekly breakfast, or a monthly dinner. Just be consistent.
- **Expose all weakness.** Make sure your accountability partner knows where you're weak, and consistently ask one another about your vulnerable areas.
- **Express all goals.** As God reveals your Chazown, share details of your developing plan.
- **Pray for one another.** Never rely on your own abilities. Always invite God to perfect His work in each of you.

Now go find the person who will hold you accountable. If the person is not your spouse, you need to choose someone of your gender.

Once you've found your accountability partner and coordinated a plan, record the details (who, when, where, what you'll do).

For more resources, visit www.chazown.com.

END MATTER

75

ALREADY LIVING WITH REGRETS?

I've experienced many regrets. I regret the way I've treated some people. I regret many things I have said. I regret times that I blatantly sinned against God. I regret missed opportunities. I regret lying, gossiping, stealing, cheating, lusting, backbiting, envying, cussing, and hating.

Regret. What a pain.

Many people with whom I talk are filled with sorrow from their past. Maybe you are living with regret right now.

If only I could have held my marriage together. I never knew pain like this before.

If only I had taken better care of my body. Who would have thought I'd end up like this?

It seemed like a good idea at the time. That decision cost me more than I ever dreamed.

I should have spent more time with the kids. They grew up way too fast. I'll never get those moments back.

Obviously we cannot change the past. We can, however, experience God's comfort, healing, and forgiveness in the present.

God specializes in loving people through regrets. And it's never too late.

Perhaps it is time to go to God honestly. Confess your sins and regrets to Him. Don't hold back. Let it loose. Cry if you feel like it. Shout if you need to. Release your hurt and pain. He is listening. And He cares.

If you are a follower of Christ, you've heard that God has forgiven you. For a great reminder, meditate on God's words from Psalm 103:11–12: "As high as the heavens are above the earth, so great is his love for those who fear him; as far as the east is from the west, so far has he removed our transgressions from us."

Embrace the truth that God has forgiven your sins. Your slate is clean.

But what if you know you're not a Christ-follower? Or maybe you're not sure.

Maybe you don't feel you deserve forgiveness. Guess what? You are right. You don't deserve it. And neither do I. That is what makes God so incredible.

In His love for us, He offers us something we could never earn and don't deserve. He sent His Son, Jesus Christ, who lived a perfect and sinless life. Then He shed innocent blood on a cross as the permanent sacrifice for the forgiveness of our sins. On the third day, He rose from the dead.

If there had been another way for us to be right with God, Jesus would not have had to become a man, die, and be raised.

Because of His perfect work, you can be forgiven. So go to Him and drop your guard. First John 1:9 says, "If we confess our sins, he is faithful and just and will forgive us our sins and purify us from all unrighteousness."

Call on Jesus to be the Lord and Savior of your life. Decide to follow Him. Become a disciple of Christ.

If you have confessed your sins to God, you are forgiven. God does not remember your sins. You become a new person.

And since God has forgiven you, maybe it's time you forgave yourself.

YES, BUT…

A friend of mine said to me, "So I'm forgiven by God—that's great! But my life is still a mess. If God has a Chazown for me to live, how can I recover from all these mistakes?"

No one can blame you for wondering, *Have I blown it too big? Is it too late for me? How can I get past all the bad things I have done?*

I'd love to tell you all your problems can immediately go away. That would be a lie. The truth is, we all face consequences for our actions and bad decisions.

At the same time, listen to Romans 8:28: "We know that in all things God works for the good of those who love him, who have been called according to his purpose."

Let that sink in. Even though we will face challenges from our wrong decisions, God is still at work in everything. God has a way of bringing good from all things—even the things we regret.

That's the basis on which God deals with our "yes, buts."

Yes, I know God forgives me, but I can never be truly blessed.

Yes, I know God is good, but He won't be good to me.

Yes, I know God has a plan for others, but I have messed up too badly!

Take the "but" out of each of your "yes, buts," and replace it with an exclamation point. "Yes!" God is a big God who can bring good out of everything.

So what is this "good" God is going to produce in your messed-up life? You may have some picture of what that would be, but your picture is likely inaccurate. Let me illustrate what I mean.

I rarely drink soft drinks. Occasionally I'll take a walk on the wild side, set aside my usual H_2O, and drink a soft drink instead.

One day I approached a soft drink machine with two quarters in hand, full of anticipation for a nice, cool, refreshing Sprite. When I deposited the coins and pushed the Sprite button, a red light revealed that the machine was out of Sprite. Second best is Dr Pepper, but that supply was depleted as well. All of the regular Coke was gone too.

That left only one choice…*(shudder)*…diet.

You may like diet drinks. If you do, God can set you free. I hate them.

Disappointed that the machine didn't have my drink of choice, or first or second runners-up, I pushed the Diet Coke button.

You will never guess what came out.

Not Diet Coke. Not Sprite, Dr Pepper, or regular Coke.

I thought I knew what "good" was for me. But my picture of "good" was inaccurate. God exceeded my expectations.

Out of the machine shot…a strawberry soda! In my world, there is nothing better than a strawberry soda. God didn't give me what I wanted. He gave me an upgrade!

So go ahead and dream of the good that God will bring out of your pain and regrets. But keep your eyes open. God may have a few surprises for you. You're picturing Sprite. But in some way or another, God might give you a strawberry soda!

MY PART IS FINISHED— YOURS IS JUST BEGINNING

You've dreamed your dreams (at least some of them). You've begun to seek God and His Chazown. You're learning to examine yourself, to understand better your unique design and purpose. You've set some good goals. And you've chosen (or will choose) someone to go with you on the journey, to help you stay on the path.

You've come a long way! Great job!

But everything to this point has been prologue. Your story is only beginning. Today is the first day of the rest of your life. Your past is behind you. Your future is in God's hands, and He's inviting you to participate actively, willingly in His Chazown for your life.

> Your story is only beginning.

Remember, you were created by God for His glory and purpose. He could have placed you at any moment in history. But He chose for you to live today. Why? Because today is the best time in the existence of the world for you to make a difference.

Are you ready?

You began this book by writing your final chapter—the epitaph for your life.

Now turn the page.

It's time for you to start writing your first chapter...

YOU'RE THE AUTHOR

My Chapter One

CHAZOWN CONVERSATIONS

A Study Guide for Personal and Group Use

Most of us need to process major life decisions aloud, preferably with others who are on the same journey. And Chazown is all about major life decisions! You probably need time to ponder, evaluate, problem-solve and decide. That's why we've included this conversation guide in this updated edition of the book. This guide is not meant to replace your personal investment in the "You're the Author" assignments in the book, or "The Chazown Experience" that is available online (www.chazown.com). But if you're serious about defining and pursuing your life purpose with passion, you'll benefit from thinking and talking your way through the questions that follow.

You'll see that "Chazown Conversations" presents the sixteen learning units of *Chazown* in a **four-week format**. Church classes and small groups may find this approach most convenient for their schedules. Individuals and small groups who are working through the book at their own pace can simply ignore the "Week" designations, and follow the **chapter-by-chapter format**.

Don't forget to take advantage of the resources at www.chazown.com, and the two new appendixes in this edition: "Learning from Past Experiences" and "Clarifying Your Core Values and Spiritual Gifts."

God bless you as you define your vision, pursue your passion, and live your life on purpose for His glory!

WEEK ONE

Why you need a new kind of vision. Where to look for your own Chazown, starting with your core values and spiritual gifts.

Part One: Seeing Clear to the End (pages 1–16)

1. Imagine—a book about your life that start's with your death! What good can come of that? Is it biblical? Spark any new thoughts or feelings for you?

2. Would you say that you *do* feel uniquely created by a loving God for a purpose, or not? How do your growing up experiences or your present circumstances affect your answer?

3. Craig says "few people end up somewhere on purpose." How much would you say your life so far has been defined by purpose? A) a lot, B) quite a lot, or C) not much at all? Explain.

4. Talk about what you wrote for your epitaph. Did anything become clear to you that hadn't been before, or that you haven't thought about for a long time? What would have to change for you to begin to do something about it?

Part Two: Circling the Truth (pages 17–24)

5. Have you been waiting for a supernatural sign to show you God's purpose for your life? If so, like what? As Craig says, God can show you His vision for you any way and anytime He pleases. If you haven't already, why not ask God right now to use your study of Chazown to show you His Chazown for you.

Circle One: Core Values (pages 25–40)

6. What do you cherish at your core? Write it down. How much does what you cherish direct how you are investing your time and energy these days?

7. What makes you angry? What brings you bliss? What do your answers show you about yourself that you may not be taking seriously enough?

Circle Two: Spiritual Gifts (pages 41–51)

8. In the "Keira, Red with Pie" story, which friend would you say best describes you, and why?

9. Talk about your written answers on "You're the Author: Your Spiritual Gifts." What did God seem to show you as you thought through this personal inventory?

WEEK TWO

Rethinking your past experiences, naming your Chazown, and making a plan to move from vision to action.

Circle Three: Past Experiences (pages 52–59)

1. It's easy for most Christians to see God in *some* of our past experiences. But there are always at least a few that seem random, pointless, and unredeemable. Do you have one or more of those experiences in your past? Can you talk about them? Ask God to include them in the "all things" that He works together for good—and begin to change how you value them in your own life.

2. Do your good and bad experiences have a thread in common? If so, what does it seem to show about you as a person?

Part Three: A Dream in Deed (pages 61–68)

3. In this reading, you arrived at your "sweet spot"—where the circles of your core values, spiritual gifts, and past experiences overlap. Did you make a personal breakthrough here, or are you still processing?

4. Finish this sentence, "God has created me with a dream for my life, and I think it might be _____ _____."

Naming Your Chazown (pages 69–79)

    5. Talk about your answer to this question: "If money were not object and I could do anything I wanted for the rest of my life, what would I do?"

    6. Craig says that God will call you to something you *can't* do on your own. Why would God do that, in your opinion?

Moving from Vision to Action (pages 80–93)

    7. Are you good at planning? Okay at it? Terrible at it? Talk about your answer, and how your approach to planning has impacted your life.

    8. When it comes to writing out the specifics of a goal and an action plan to achieve that goal, plenty of people find themselves getting anxious, doubtful, or overcome by a desire to delay. How did you feel?

WEEK THREE

Identifying five life areas that define success. Setting your small "c" chazown goals for your relationship with God, your relationships with people, and your finances.

Part Four: The Five Spokes of Chazown (pages 95–108)

    1. Craig asks a haunting question: "Why do so many gifted people self-destruct? Everything on the outside of their lives can look so good. But something unseen isn't right." What are your thoughts as you read this?

    2. Have you ever taken a comprehensive look at the major areas of your life—Craig calls them spokes—and considered how they need to all work together? Which of the spokes *Chazown* will tackle (God, people, finances, work, health) are you most concerned might be "loose" in your life?

First Spoke: Relationship with God (pages 109–122)

3. Hot, cold, or lukewarm—how would you describe the temperature of your heart for God right now? Looking back, do you see changes in that temperature over months or years? If so, do the changes bother or encourage you?

4. Craig describes the basic spiritual disciplines that help us live close to God's heart—Bible study, prayer, fasting, worship, fellowship with other believers, accountability, service, and outreach. In which of these areas are you doing well? Which just okay? Which not well at all?

5. What's the next step you will take to reach your goal in this area?

Second Spoke: Relationships with People (pages 123–142)

6. Would you say that you have maintained relationships well in your life? Or would you say that you haven't done so well at this, and important relationships have fallen away or ended?

7. Do any relationships in your life need to be restored? Do any need to be ended? What goal-oriented steps will you take?

Third Spoke: Finances (pages 143–162)

8. Craig writes, "Every one of us is susceptible to bondage to money—a millionaire as much as a homeless person." In what ways has money been a challenge in your life? What do you sense God is asking you to change in how you relate to and manage your finances?

9. Did you get started on developing your financial action plan (described in "You're the Author: Your Finances")? If not, what's holding you back, and how could you get past that obstacle? If so, what's a next important step for you to take?

WEEK FOUR

Setting goals for life areas four and five—health and fitness, and work. Deciding not to quit. Building your accountability plan and putting your team in place. And finally, letting go of pain, regrets, and limiting expectations.

Fourth Spoke: Health and Fitness (pages 163–178)

1. When it comes to health and fitness, our minds are jam packed with mental excuses and what Craig calls "easy lies." What kinds of misleading self-talk have been the most problematic for you?

2. Craig writes that God has made us managers, not owners, over our bodies. Based on your actions over the last month, would you say that you are behaving more like a manager or more like an owner?

Fifth Spoke: Work (pages 179–191)

3. Talk about what your family of origin taught you in word and example about work. For example, what was the driving value—money, security, helping people, necessity, perseverance, something to be avoided? How have those values affected your own choices? Which values do you want to change?

4. Would you say your work life—what you do with most of your time—is an expression of your Chazown or something less? What changes are you ready to make?

Part Five: From Here to Eternity (pages 193–212)

5. As you wrap up your exploration of the Three Circles and Five Spokes of your Chazown, how are you feeling: overwhelmed or energized? fearful or confident? cautious or optimistic? confused or clear-minded?

6. Until now have you thought that your success was all up to you, or have you operated intentionally with support and accountability?

Talk about the practical, specific steps you plan to take to put your Chazown success team in place.

End Matter (pages 213–219)

7. How much do pain and regret affect your daily life now, and what do you think God probably has in mind for your future? If you would say "a lot," how did you respond to Craig's invitation to give all of it—pain, regret, and expectations—over to God?

8. How are you feeling now about pursuing your life purpose with passion? What actions will be different today as a result? What outcomes can you expect, by your effort and God's grace, to be different in the future?

APPENDIX A

Learning from Past Experiences

P ast experiences are events or seasons in your life that prepare you for the purpose and vision God has planned for you.

To help you begin to see God's Chazown in your past experiences, you are going to create something unique: *a Personal Time Line*. Your time line is a big-picture overview of your life that will help you begin to see God's Chazown for your life.

CREATING A PERSONAL TIME LINE

To create your time line, you will need:
- One standard poster board, cut in half
- Four colors of small sticky notes (preferably yellow, pink, blue, and green)
- A pen

Step One: Identify the People, Events, and Circumstances that have Most Affected Your Life

Using your yellow sticky notes, begin to write down the **key people**, **events**, and **circumstances** that have shaped your life up to this point. Use a separate sticky note for each one. Include both good and difficult moments.

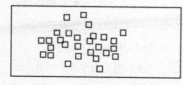 As you complete this step, it is important to "brainstorm" and allow your mind to roam freely. Remember, the only rule of brainstorming is that there are no wrong answers! As soon as a name, an important event, or a life circumstance comes to mind, write a one or two word name or description down

on a sticky note. Peel it off, place on the table you are working on, and write another. (Don't place them on the poster board yet). *By the end of this exercise, you should have twenty to thirty sticky notes providing a cross-section of the significant details of your life story.*

- The **key people** who influenced and shaped your life may include friends, family members, classmates, work associates, peers, mentors, pastors, your spouse, teachers, church friends and acquaintances, and others.
- The **events** that have impacted your life may include graduation, awards, projects you worked on, jobs you've held, changes in the community, global events that had a personal impact on you, job loss, and other defining moments.
- The significant **circumstances** that have affected your life direction may include places you lived, career demands of your parents, early childhood experiences, schools you attended, ministries you were involved in, and retreats you experienced—among other things.

Step Two: Putting Things in Order

Next, you will organize your sticky notes chronologically.

Place a sticky note at the very top and the very bottom of the poster board and mark both with a big "X." The purpose of these "X" notes is to remind you that when you place your sticky notes on your board, you should leave a margin across the top and the bottom that is the width of one sticky note. To do this, you will need to place your yellow notes in the space between these two "X" notes.

Organize your sticky notes chronologically. Place your earliest sticky note in the top left corner (remembering to leave room for the margin across the top of your poster board.) Place your second earliest sticky note below the first note. Continue to place your notes on the poster board, proceeding in a vertical column down the left side until you reach the bottom (remembering to leave room for the margin across the bottom). Return to the top of your board and continue the process in columns until all of your sticky notes are placed in chronological order.

Step Three: Calling It Like It Was

Once you have finished, take a moment and look at all of the sticky notes on your board. Ask yourself which of them were painful or hurtful when you ex-

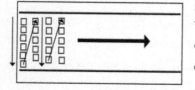

perienced them. As you identify those that were difficult, transfer what you wrote on the original yellow note to a pink sticky note and discard the yellow one.

You may wonder why your most difficult experiences are being singled out during this exercise. The act of changing the color of the sticky note for the difficult or hurtful experiences allows you to consciously say to yourself, "This one was difficult…that one hurt." God does some of his deepest work through some of our most difficult moments in life. It is important to acknowledge those times and seasons.

Step Four: Organize Your Time Line into Chapters

Now take several moments and look at the notes assembled on your poster

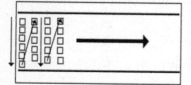

board. As you do, you will probably see key segments, or "chapters" of your life journey begin to emerge. Try to identify no fewer than three and no more than six chapters. As you identify these chapters, you may need to move your sticky notes around some to reflect those chapters.

Using the blue sticky notes, write down titles for the chapters you have identified and place them along the top margin of your poster board above the chapter they represent. Your chapter titles should reflect your thoughts and feelings about what was occurring in your life during that chapter. Fcel free to be creative as you choose titles that reflect you. Some participants have used popular movie titles, while others have chosen names that center around a favorite hobby or sport. You may also choose terms that may seem random or meaningless to someone else, but that are personally very significant. The important thing is to choose titles that mean something to you. It's your life story!

Step Five: Clarify the Turning Points and Major Lessons

Next, you will identify the "turning points" in your time line. A turning point is an event, experience, or encounter that altered your life. It is a defining moment in your journey when:

- Life changed for better or worse
- Someone intervened in a significant way
- An important decision was made
- You moved in a new direction
- Anything else that impacted you in a meaningful and lasting way

Turning points are characterized by the fact that in some way, life was not the same after the experience. God deposits key insights and develops character in us at the turning points of life. Identifying them will help you see the important lessons you've learned along the way.

Take several moments and examine your time line again, looking for six to eight turning points; the events, experiences, and encounters that have altered your life in important ways. Once you have identified them, boldly write "TP" on the top of those sticky notes.

Spend a few moments reflecting on each turning point. Think about why each is important. You may want to talk about them with a friend, mentor, or family member.

Now, using the green sticky notes, write down lessons and themes that emerge through your life chapters and turning points. You may want to use the following questions as a guide:

- What was God trying to teach me during this chapter or turning point of my life?
- What should I remember as I move forward?
- What abilities or insights has God deposited into my life as a result of this experience?
- In what ways can the skills or insights God gave me through this experience impact my future?

- What character traits were developed in me as a result?
- What character traits have I come to value most in others?
- Are there any unique experiences or insights I have gained?
- What are some of the ways God used me?
- Did this experience reveal anything to me about what God is like?

Place these lessons and themes along the bottom margin of your poster board, underneath the corresponding turning point or chapter. Then list them in the circle below.

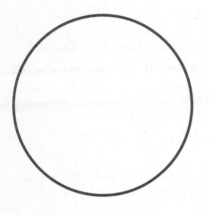

These major lessons and themes will help God's plan for your life come into focus and will play a key role in the discovery of your personal Chazown!

For additional help and resources related to creating a personal time line and how God shapes and develops each of our lives for a unique contribution, contact Leader Breakthru and Terry Walling at www.leaderbreakthru.com.

Leader Breakthru offers coaching, resources, and training that facilitate breakthrough in the lives of risk-taking kingdom leaders.

APPENDIX B

Clarifying Your Core Values and Spiritual Gifts

WHAT ARE YOUR CORE VALUES?

When God made you, He planted within you certain things you value deeply. They're hardwired into your heart. Through your life experiences, God has begun to make them clear to you. These are the things you would be willing to die for. They explain how you come by your personal priorities. We will call these things your **core values**.

> Our responsibility is never to oppose the truth, but to stand for the truth at all times. (2 Corinthians 13:8, NLT)

To identify your core values, it may help to ask yourself the following questions:
- What stirs righteous anger inside of you?
- What makes you especially happy?
- Does your personal time line tell you anything about your core values?

Below are some examples of the core values you may possess. Use the following list as a guide, circling any that may apply to you. Add others that come to mind if they are not listed here.

Accountability	Compassion
Attitude	Confidence
Authenticity	Courage
Boldness	Creativity
Character	Dedication
Collaboration	Devotion

Discipleship
Discipline
Discovery
Diversity
Efficiency
Encouragement
Endurance
Enthusiasm
Evangelism
Excellence
Faith
Faithfulness
Family
Fellowship
Generosity
Gentleness
Godliness
Goodness
Grace
Gratefulness
Growth
Honesty
Honor
Hope
Humility
Humor
Integrity
Intimacy
Joy
Justice
Kindness
Knowing God
Leadership
Learning

Loyalty
Mercy
Obedience
Openness
Order
Passion
Patience
Peace
Perseverance
Personal Growth
Prayer
Purity
Relationships
Reliability
Respect
Sacrifice
Self-control
Self-discipline
Selflessness
Servant Leadership
Servanthood
Steadfastness
Stewardship
Submission
Teachability
Teamwork
Thankfulness
Transparency
Trustworthiness
Truth
Unity
Wisdom
Worship
Zeal

Now that you have circled the values that apply to you, pray and ask God to guide you as you narrow this list down even further. As you pray, continue to ask yourself, "What makes me angry with a righteous anger?" and "What do I absolutely love, more than anything else?" Try to focus your list to between five and ten core values and list them in the circle below.

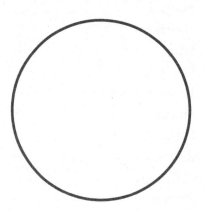

Think of a personal story or experience that coincides with each of the core values you have identified. Consider sharing these stories with someone important to you. As you begin to live, walk, and talk about your core values, you will begin to move closer to the Chazown God has in mind for you!

WHAT ABOUT YOUR SPIRITUAL GIFTS?

Just as your core values were planted in you by God, so were your spiritual gifts.

> We have different gifts, according to the grace given us. (Romans 12:6)

These gifts are especially chosen for the Chazown to which He is calling you.

The Bible has several lists of talents and abilities, but these are only samplings of a much longer unwritten "list" of gifts that God has distributed throughout humanity.

To determine which of these gifts God has specifically gifted you with, go online and visit www.chazown.com. There you can take an assessment that will help identify your spiritual gifts.

Once you have completed a spiritual-gifts assessment, prayerfully consider the results. Do you feel they accurately reflect your gifts? Are there other things you or others have identified that you are especially good at?

Once you have answered these questions, ask God to use your answers to reveal your spiritual gifts. List your spiritual gifts in the circle below.

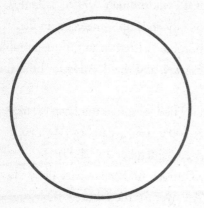

Your spiritual gifts reveal a lot about the plans God has for you. Knowing how God has gifted you moves you one step closer to understanding the Chazown He has planned for your life!

NOTES

1. Andy Stanley, *Visioneering* (Sisters, OR: Multnomah, 1999), 8. Andy's wording is slightly different. ("Everybody ends up somewhere in life. A few people end up somewhere on purpose.") I return to this memorable statement often in the course of *Chazown,* and thank Andy for both the idea and for his outstanding book.

2. D. L. Moody quoted in Luis Palau, "The Destiny of the Lost," *Reaching Your World with Luis Palau,* July 15, 2005, www.palau.org/ryw_new/scripts.php?date=2005-17-15 (accessed September 28, 2005).

3. Sir Francis Drake, quoted in Jeanie Curryer, OC Missionary Prayer Letter, September 1997. Retrieved from "A Prayer for the Future," Bible.org, http://bible.org/illustration/prayer-future (accessed April 17, 2010).

4. See Genesis 37, 39.

5. See Genesis 40–50.

6. See Matthew 21:12–13 and John 2:14–16.

7. See Matthew 23.

8. See Matthew 26:31–35, 69–75.

9. See 1 Samuel 17, especially verses 34–37.

10. See Matthew 16:21–23.

11. See 1 Corinthians 3:16; 6:19.

12. See Luke 6:13.

13. See also Ephesians 4:32.

14. Paul Billheimer, quoted in "Finance (Life After Debt)," BibleUniverse.com, www.bibleuniverse.com/finance/finance.asp (accessed October 7, 2005).

15. See, for example, Exodus 23:16, 19; Proverbs 3:9–10.

16. John Maxwell, *Today Matters* (New York: Warner Faith, 2004), 89.

17. Ron Fimrite, *Sports Illustrated,* quoted in "Habits," SermonIllustrations.com, www.sermonillustrations.com/a-z/h/habits.htm (accessed April 23, 2010).

18. See also Matthew 12:36; 2 Corinthians 5:10.

ACKNOWLEDGMENTS

To the many who provided help, encouragement, and expertise during the process of getting the *Chazown* message in print, I am sincerely grateful. Thank you for your generosity.

I'm especially indebted to

- Brian Smith—Your encouragement, creativity, writing, and vision made this book possible. Even more than our hard hours of working together, I'll remember and always value our friendship.
- the whole Multnomah team, including David Kopp, Jason Myhre, Kevin Marks, Jake Burts, Doug Gabbert, David Webb, Katherine Lloyd, and James Hall, among many others—You are tenacious in your pursuit of godly excellence. Thanks for your kingdom partnership and friendship.
- my LifeChurch.tv family—Thank you for believing. God is good!
- Amy and my children—You are everything to me.

Love, sex, and happily ever after?

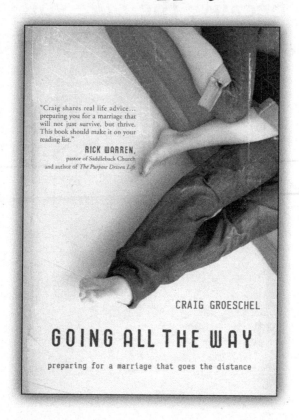

"Craig shares real life advice... preparing you for a marriage that will not just survive, but thrive. This book should make it on your reading list."

RICK WARREN,
pastor of Saddleback Church
and author of *The Purpose Driven Life*

CRAIG GROESCHEL

GOING ALL THE WAY

preparing for a marriage that goes the distance

"Going all the way" used to mean getting what you want from the opposite sex now...and paying for it later. It's time to redefine.

Whether you're thinking ahead to marriage, are about to be wed, or have been married for a while and want to make changes, Craig Groeschel's *Going All the Way* will guide you through the choices and commitments you need to make now in order to build a strong and vibrant relationship that will go the distance.

Is the *real* you getting lost because the *fake* you is just so annoyingly impressive?

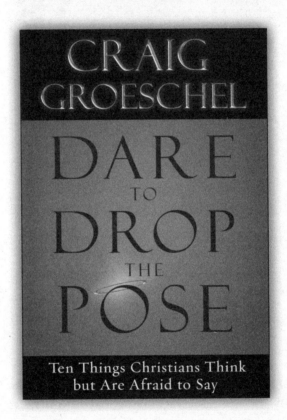

Why *do* we fake it so much? Why do we spend so much time trying to please everyone and make so little effort trying to please God? When Craig Groeschel asked himself those questions, he couldn't come up with a good answer. So he decided to drop the act—and his life began to change in a big way. In *Dare to Drop the Pose* Groeschel unmasks the dark side of life, and provides real hope to help you find authentic living and a deeper relationship with God.